Secrets of the Skim

Secrets of the Skim

A Merrill Lynch financial advisor's tale of the raw greed and cultural rot harbored in the belly of Wall Street's most iconic institutional beast. For the first time the true agenda of America's wealth management industry is revealed!

Hal Blackwell

Dedicated to my girls, Anita, Vowan and Claire.

Contents

Preface   IX

Introduction   XIII

Main Characters   XIX

1. A New Calling   1

2. Pledging the Fraternity   9

3. Fifteen-Million-Dollar Mountain   17

4. Put Me In, Coach   23

5. The Politics of Fear   29

6. Rules of the Road   39

7. Getting Lucky   55

8. Mister Big Stuff   65

9. Flying Blind   73

10. Eminence Front   79

11. Cauldron   85

12. The Prediction   93

13. Conviction to Act   101

14. A New Deal   111

15. Revelation   121

16. The Pecan Brief   129

17. Brush with Death   135

18. Up on the Hill   139

19. Standing My Ground   151

20. Somewhere Down the Track   155

21. Before the Court   163

22. Epilogue   177

Addendum   xxx

About the Author   181

Merrill Lynch U-5 Form   183

Hal Blackwell's letter to FINRA in response to the
Merrill Lynch accusations   187

Preface

To make this book effective I had to be completely candid regarding some of my personal character flaws. But that was not the hard part. The hard part was disclosing facts that will embarrass some of my former colleagues. I have concluded this story must be told because changing the wealth management industry is vital to preserving America's economic freedom.

When I left Merrill Lynch, shocked and disgusted at my treatment, I did not see the parting as a blessing. But in His perfect wisdom, God had decided to intervene. As days have passed, the perfection of the timing has become clear. On the day I was fired, September 16, 2009, the obligation to my largest project, Ag Renewable Fuels, had been met after eighteen months of striving. God has a way of turning perceived disaster into brand new horizons. Indeed, His timing was perfect.

The game that wealth management firms have played over the years has turned into a perverted process akin to larceny, and my aim is to change that. My apathy has been vanquished, and my dreams are big. For a person who hails from a small textile town in upstate South Carolina and has labored only on the edges of this most powerful economic force, my odds are long. Truth and destiny are my allies now, and we hope to recruit our readers into a vast legion of patriots. We shall grab the initiative and not relent.

In the fall of 2008, when the federal government bailed out the banks designated "too big to fail," the U.S. financial system was nationalized. By deeming certain financial institution as deserving of backing by the United States Treasury, all other characteristics of these organizations became peripheral. Logically, since the taxpayer is at risk, the Congress will impose restrictions on these institutions. Whether or not the government holds shares in these institutions is not relevant. The government will forever be perceived as the cosigner for these titans of Wall Street. A rose by any other name…

In the current economic climate, this seems an unfair advantage for the too-big-to-fail banks, and it is. But this can be a double-edged sword. For nearly a hundred years the U.S. dollar has enjoyed an exalted status not shared with any other currency. If, however, the momentum of the never-ending federal fiscal largesse eventually brings down "King Dollar," these Wall Street firms will find their sugar daddy, Uncle Sam, to be the source of their undoing. The banks' savior of 2008 will be in need of a rescue of his own, and both players will be powerless to forestall a day of reckoning.

If free enterprise is to ever return the U.S. economy to competitiveness, these institutions must be broken into "failable" pieces. Banks must not be permitted to gain too-big-to-fail status, just as the monopolies of the late nineteenth century were legislated out of existence. Such legislative action is one of the few proper functions of government.

The government has assumed unprecedented power on Wall Street, and dislodging it now will require historic action. This is not the late nineteenth century, and a modern-day Teddy Roosevelt is nowhere in sight. This time around, the managers of these institutions find themselves in a strange alliance with their traditional adversaries (power-hungry politicians and regulators) in maintaining the status quo. To dismantle the lucrative ivory towers from which these global power-players squeeze dollars year after year will require a grassroots intervention.

It is my prayer that after reading this book the reader will be aware of how important these issues are to the survival of our republic.

The retribution I am sure to suffer as a result of exposing the misdeeds of very powerful people and their sacred institutions will be worn as a badge of honor. Many of the names used in this book are fictional to protect the guilty as well as the innocent. Only the real names of upper management at Merrill Lynch are used. The others will be spared Google searches because they are only symptoms of the problem. They are given this consideration because in a strange twist they themselves are victims. Their perception of reality has been skewed by the intentional and effective brainwashing that is part and parcel of an industry in which a successful career is spent dulling the conscience in pursuit of money.

At this crucial juncture in our history, the American culture and economy are in desperate need of patriots. I hope this book will be accepted as my small contribution to embolden change at this critical time when America's future is being determined. The rectitude of the struggle cannot be measured by the power of the forces in opposition.

Introduction

How much cash do you have in your pocket, or in your car, or at home? In the fall of 2008, that very nearly became the ultimate question for the unsuspecting American masses. The U.S. financial system's liquidity was evaporating at such a rapid pace that Secretary of the Treasury Hank Paulson and Federal Reserve Board Chairman Ben Bernanke were frantically seeking to keep American debit cards and checks clearing the system. When the bankruptcy of Lehman Brothers caused the Primary Reserve Money Market fund to "break the buck," the safest investments in our economy were at risk. Paulson and Bernanke were desperately trying to ensure that companies in our economy like Wal-Mart and McDonald's were going to be able to make payroll. The failure of their mission would have resulted in an anarchy dwarfing the events of the Great Depression.

In the 1930s, a drain of liquidity precipitated, and then exacerbated, a run on banks, contributing to the Great Depression. Eighty years later, consumers faced the possibility of being electronically robbed of their purchasing power. The populace, becoming indigent at the speed of light, would have started a run on the supermarkets. Food riots are ugly and violent. Paulson and Bernanke knew American society might not be capable of recovering from the specter of marauding bands of the hungry taking food from wherever it might be found.

Very few people realize how close to the brink the global financial system stood in the fall of 2008. Equally misunderstood are the implications of what would have occurred had we fallen over that brink and into the financial abyss. The fabric of our society, the rule of law, could not have survived. Making statements like this can quickly get one labeled as hysterical or prone to exaggeration. That's one reason the public has not been educated about the gravity of the situation. The other more primary reason no one has come forth to speak this way is that there is no "upside" in doing so. Politicians know reelection campaigns are not aided by admitting to the gravity of one's neglect. Leaders in the business community realize they are in enough trouble as it is. The media is asleep at the switch or too involved in promoting a political agenda to take up the cause.

Many questions have arisen as a result of the events that preceded the near collapse, but nearly all have been superficial. The pertinent and foundational questions have not been asked, much less answered.

The investing public has a right to know the specifics of what the leaders of the U.S. financial institutions knew and when they knew it. In late August 2008, did Merrill Lynch chairman and CEO John Thain understand the depth of the crisis? Either he was mega stupid, or he and his cadre made a decision not to advise the retail clients of Merrill Lynch about the perils to their life savings just around the corner. Thain (as well as Lloyd Blankfein, Dick Fuld, Vikram Pandit, and John Mack) had a fiduciary responsibility to the firm's clients to be forthcoming. Claiming ignorance of the situation does not jive with the facts, but it seems to be the popular strategy employed to dodge culpability.

No, the truth is more disturbing than anyone on Wall Street, in Washington, or in the media wants to contemplate. The truth is that these men could not fulfill the fiduciary obligation to their clients because to do so would have pushed the world into an economy worse than the Great Depression. The crime was not so much the failure to live up to their responsibility but the acts of greed that created the circumstance.

As a financial advisor at Merrill Lynch during this time, it became clear that senior management made a decision to keep the Thundering Herd[1] in the dark. "More shoes to drop" was the phrase management used to acknowledge there was trouble ahead, without providing any further elaboration.

The 2008 first quarter earnings report for Merrill Lynch showed a dreadful $2 billion loss. The subsequent communiqué from management was that the worst was over, but there might be "more shoes to drop." Again in July when the second quarterly report showed a whopping $4.6 billion loss, the "more shoes to

---

[1] The Thundering Herd is the nickname of the financial advisors at Merrill Lynch.

drop" refrain had become an all too familiar song. The song was sung after the sale of assets to Lone Star for pennies on the dollar, the dilution of shares to raise capital, or anytime the plummeting stock price was mentioned. Every episode was followed by the words "the worst is over, but there may be more shoes to drop." The management I interacted with steadfastly refused to speculate on whether the "shoes" belonged to Tom Thumb or Paul Bunyan.

Policymakers, so intently focused on bringing the investment bankers into line, are willing to give these guys a pass on the neglect of their de facto fiduciary responsibility in the midst of the crisis. Because articulating the situation to financial advisors might have caused a self-fulfilling panic, no clatter has been made of this malfeasance. These decision makers are not lawmakers, and their refusal to live up to the standards set by Constitutional jurisprudence is not to be ignored. The arrogance and an "entitlement" attitude of the men and women perched atop our most sacred financial institutions are the products of an industry with a corrupt soul. Denying the depth of the problem only perpetuates a growing venerability within the U.S. wealth management institutions.

This "soul sickness" is never more clearly apparent than when the industry's marketing strategy is examined from the perspective of the image it attempts to create.

An *image* is different from a *brand*.

A brand is an ideology that permeates an organization. Channeled from the highest levels of management down to the mailroom clerks, corporate venders, and all who implement the mission statement, a brand creates organizational identity.

An image diverges from a brand when the public perception of a corporate identity does not mesh with the corporation's perception. An image turns into a façade and confidence game when it is carefully crafted to hide the real objectives of an organization. The financial services industry in our country is not designed to meet its fiduciary responsibility to the clients it serves, contrary to the message of the hired guns of the Madison Avenue media machine.

The financial services industry in the United States has spent billions of dollars crafting a deceptive image.

The methods used by these peddlers of investment products over the decades have firmly entrenched a culture in the towers of Wall Street that functions in conflict with the interests of the client. Techniques to engender public trust are designed to separate the unsuspecting investor from his hard-earned money under false pretenses.

The firms that spend millions of dollars creating these images have a hidden agenda. While they superficially reach out to unsuspecting investors, the real targets are the high-revenue-producing financial advisors who in reality drive the industry. The slick ad campaigns are part of the platform of services touted by these firms to lure big-dog brokers into the fold.

This hidden agenda has fostered the creation of a culture that incentivizes management to corral the slickest "backslappers" who have perfected underhanded techniques to generate revenue for the firm. Competent financial managers dedicated to the fiduciary responsibility owed their clients are viewed as disillusioned byproducts, the cost of doing business, a drag on corporate earnings.

Nobody begrudges financial advisors who are paid with disclosed fees and commissions. The ability of firms in this industry to earn undisclosed fees (or to bury the disclosure so deep in an ocean of paper that Kreskin couldn't find it) has created a parasitic culture detrimental to the investors it serves and the economy in which it operates.

This book seeks to reveal the methods used by these financial institutions and the callous greed that has enriched undeserving impostors at the expense of hard-working entrepreneurs, retirees and widows, or anyone else with a dollar to invest. More importantly, this book seeks to illustrate the particular nature of this culture in hopes that those in a position to remedy the wrongs will do so at a level deep enough to be effective.

The lesson of our present financial crisis is that our current regulatory paradigm is ineffective in combating cultural greed on a modern scale. Legislators must focus their efforts on constructing rules and guidelines that require transparency. The marketplace must be the final arbiter of who is moral and who is not. Our legislators must change their focus from seeking power through regulatory authority to requiring transparency at all levels of our nation's financial infrastructure, including the Federal Reserve.

This book does not list the mundane litany of abuses of the industry because it is pointless to dwell on the symptoms of the disease. The disease that must be addressed is the industry's culture. *Secrets of the Skim* tells a story that puts these abuses in context. My experiences at Merrill Lynch melted my naïveté to reveal the wealth management industry's core issues as never before seen by the investing public.

As I recount my industry experiences, no punches are pulled and no quarter is given. The chips must fall where they may so that our economy, our society, and our country can be rescued from this culture of corruption. My experience is not unique. The story about to be told happens every day in just about every city across this nation.

Because disclosure of the industry's schemes is too important to let it remain hidden solely to spare personal embarrassment, the good guys in the industry, and there are many, must take the hit along with their less ethical colleagues.

Main Characters

(f) denotes fictional name of a real person, real place or real company

Merrill Lynch, Blueberg (f), South Carolina

Hank Patton (f)
Blueberg office manager

Sam Reagan (f)
Financial advisor

Reggie Sparks (f)
Financial advisor

Mike Bling (f)
Financial advisor

Ted Tiller (f)
Financial advisor

Harley Johnson (f)
Financial advisor

Rudy Mantooth (f)
Financial advisor

Richard Rutledge (f)
Financial advisor

Tom Hawkins (f)
Financial advisor

Emily Smith (f)
Financial advisor

Herb Camp (f)
Financial advisor

Nick Neapolitan (f)
Financial advisor

Elaine Massey (f)
Client associate

Hassy Meadows (f)
Client associate

Lucy Stone (f)
Client associate

Rikki Jakes (f)
Client Associate

Bill Mitchell (f)
Financial advisor and new office manager after Hank Patton

Merrill Lynch, Blueberg (f), South Carolina, post-merger

Flip Hebert (f)
Financial advisor

Roger Kendrick (f)
Financial advisor

Jack Haley (f)
Financial advisor

Wells Stewart (f)
Financial advisor

Merrill Lynch, Pleasantburg (f), South Carolina

Paul Pressley (f)
Financial advisor and coach for new hires

Merrill Lynch Management, Charlotte, North Carolina

Randy Dennis (f)
Administrator working for Don Plaus, Merrill Lynch

Frank Frazer
Complex Business Manager

Don Minor
Compliance officer before merger with Bank of America

Don Plaus
Complex manager until merger, promoted to regional manager

Scott Hotham
Complex manager before and after Don Plaus

Merrill Lynch Management, Columbia, South Carolina

Bill Edmunds
Office manager, post-merger

Kyle Rice
Complex compliance officer

Ag Renewable Fuels (f)

Derek Cannon (f)
Advisor to ARF

Brock Morgan (f)
Chairman of the board after Dr. Snipes

Fontaine Capital (f)

Mosh Singho (f)

Smith Barney, Blueberg (f), South Carolina

Dick Plum (f)
Office manager

1. A New Calling

Out of the blue and into the black
You pay for this, but they give you that
And once you're gone, you can't come back
When you're out of the blue and into the black.

– Neil Young

Throughout the winter and spring of 2004, after selling the insurance agency I had nurtured for ten years in Clemson, South Carolina, I spent my days tending 370 acres of land on the Broad River in Cherokee County, South Carolina, which had been in my family since before the War Between the States. Due to my father's illness, responsibility for the place fell to me. After a twenty-year absence, the remoteness of the locale and the newness of the chores offered a once-in-a-lifetime respite to evaluate the big picture and gain some perspective.

I felt a strange attachment to the forests and river that refreshed me, and the closeness to my ancestors was palpable. The distance from my house to the property was a ninety-mile drive, mostly through lightly inhabited back roads. The winding two-lane ribbon stretched out the distance, but the length of the journey was often therapeutic.

An often taken detour from my regular drive happened to take me past the Merrill Lynch office in the little city of Blueberg, South Carolina. Considering what career path would be appropriate for my skill set had led me to think about wealth management in the financial services industry, so almost on a lark one July day I called the office and asked to schedule an interview with the manager.

To my surprise, I learned the office manager was Hank Patton, a fellow native of Folksy, a small town just east of Blueberg. That first conversation with Hank led to another, then another. I soon found myself in the Merrill Lynch office on the thirtieth floor of the Bank of America building in downtown Charlotte, North Carolina, being hosted by complex manager Scott Hotham. He was introducing me to the ways of this most fascinating society of guys and gals with mere undergraduate degrees and seven-figure annual incomes.

Scott Hotham was a serious type, not prone to small talk. With a slight build, perfectly groomed hair, and a sincere smile, he was a very imposing person in a nonthreatening way. His smallish but immaculate office overlooked Bank of America Stadium, home of the Carolina Panthers, and offered a remarkable view.

Two things about that meeting stand out in my memory. First, his telling me that in no other field he knew could a person with no postgraduate degree make the annual income he made as a matter of course. Second, my asking him if rumors that Bank of America was going to buy Merrill Lynch held any truth. His smug, cocksure answer was, "No, but we might buy them."

I doubt he remembers saying it, but the foreshadowing aspect of the comment was the dismissive arrogance with which it was uttered. There was no surprise for me in his response, but asking the question let him know my familiarity with the rumors, which was the point of my asking. I have to say I liked Scott immediately. He had a certain air of confidence that separated him from the insurance people I had been interacting with for the last twenty years. Scott Hotham was impressive, and I wanted to work for the organization he represented.

After my interview I went back to the farm. A week passed. July in South Carolina makes bush-hogging a twenty-acre field hot, sweaty, and dirty work. Riding a 1973 Ford tractor I had just acquired via an online eBay auction made it loud work as well. I'd never experienced a forty-eight-horsepower tractor's abilities, and the nature of machinery running wide open at the release of a clutch focused my attention on the high grass disappearing under the slanted front wheels grinding through the field in front of my family's old home place.

Carefully following the edge of the last cut, I made a wide turn back toward the old farmhouse and noticed my mother standing beside her car out by the road at the gate. She had brought the news that the manager of the Merrill Lynch office in Blueberg urgently needed to speak with me. Such urgency by Hank Patton had to be a good sign. Little did I suspect that I was about to step off one runaway piece of machinery onto another.

Wearing my boots, short pants, and a layer of grime, I responded to Hank's call by bringing the necessary documents to the office twenty miles away in Blueberg, as he had requested. After a short review of the documents, Hank offered me the job.

Although honored by the offer, I wanted time to think about the situation from the perspective of having the offer in hand. Hank, however, needed an answer right away and told me that he would provide the privacy of one of the glass enclosures that lined the office so that I might consult my wife. (I later learned Scott Hotham's bonus depended on Hank hiring me that afternoon. That would have been a valuable piece of information had it been available to me at the time I was negotiating my compensation and office accommodations. My hiring package would have been much improved.) I called my wife, and we decided to take the job.

Being rushed, I made several critical errors beginning my new career in the brokerage side of the financial services industry, but I am not sure I would have discovered the significance of the office pecking order even if I had researched the Merrill Lynch opportunity more thoroughly. After signing the enrollment forms, I sat with Hank in the little office where I had just called my wife. Welcoming me to Merrill Lynch, he asked me when I could start officially. I needed a couple of days to put my affairs in order, so I suggested July 27.

Hank readily agreed to my timeline, and as we stood to leave, he added with hesitation, "You do understand that you will be sitting in one of the cubicles in the beginning?"

Wanting to seem cooperative, I said, "Sure. No problem."

The office at Merrill Lynch Blueberg (MLB) consisted of a room with six cubicles in the center, surrounded by the offices of the financial advisors along the outside walls. Their assistants, called client associates or "CAs," sat right outside each advisor's door in the nearest cubicle. I realized I had gone from being the president of my company to sitting in the bullpen of Blueberg's tiny Merrill Lynch office, but I still felt good about the start of my new career. The significance of the seemingly small detail of my seating location never occurred to me until an office renovation project clued me in to the mistake I had made.

As offices go in the city of Blueberg, Merrill Lynch's location had a nice professional setting. The company name was displayed in large gold letters across the second floor of the two-story brick building. Conveniently, the office was on the first floor. A fountain out front with annuals planted around the base and a well-manicured lawn created an inviting impression for visitors.

That first day I surely felt like a visitor. I remember thinking how the office and its inhabitants would become very familiar over time, contrasting starkly with the first-day jitters I was feeling.

On my first day of work I entered the office at nine o'clock sharp, and Hank met me in the lobby with a big smile and a hearty handshake. Although he was two years my senior and his family was one of the wealthiest in Folksy, Hank and I had much in common. We knew many of the same people and had run into each other several times over the years. Following some adolescent mischief, Hank's family had sent him to boarding school in western North Carolina, but we shared a simple familiarity that I appreciated in that moment.

As we walked through the lobby's large wooden door into the inner sanctum of the office, Hank graciously acted as my guide on an introductory tour of my new home away from home. Just inside the door from the lobby was the only cube not in the center six. Here sat Hassy Meadows. Well dressed and strikingly attractive, Hassy had a firm but appropriate handshake and was very well met. She was part of a package with Richard Rutledge and Rudy Mantooth who had just come over from Blueberg's Smith Barney contingent a year earlier.

Hassy sat in the cube directly across from my new cubicle. We had no choice but to become familiar; the extent, however, was not foreseeable. I soon learned more about Hassy's personal life than I ever wanted to know, and her daily pursuit of husband number four was almost more than I could stand. The ringer on her cell phone maintained the maximum volume setting to ensure she would not miss a call, regardless of where she might be holding court in the office. This was, as I learned later, the curse of the cube that is part of the initiation requirement at Merrill Lynch.

Directly behind Hassy, Richard and Rudy shared a large office. Their space was separated from the bullpen by an attractive door and a wall that was wood-grained on the bottom and paneled glass on the top. This separate office and a subsequent renovation was part of their migration deal from Smith Barney and, as I learned later, a sign of esteem bestowed by management on only the highest-income earners.

As Hank and I walked in, Richard turned away from his computer screen and politely welcomed me to the firm, and then he immediately turned to take an incoming phone call. Rudy, who was a large man, was much nicer and took time to ask a few questions about my background and to carry on a short conversation.

Rudy seemed very likable, but something was odd about him. When he spoke niceties, his voice had a cadence. It was like he sang his words. It wasn't a southern drawl. His voice was so singsongy it had a flavor of insincerity. But he was very friendly in a political sort of way, and I appreciated his politeness.

Hank's office, of course, was in the corner. Sitting right outside his door, Elaine Massey manned the control center of the office. Though not a cube, her space could not be described as an office because it had no door. Nevertheless, her seniority was clearly displayed, and she was obviously proud of her space. The personal file cabinet, shelves on the wall, and narrow window overlooking the parking lot distinguished her locale.

Elaine had been my primary contact during the interviewing process, so I knew she was well-elevated in the pecking order. Her height, almost as tall as my five foot eleven, along with her big boned figure contrasted with a dainty voice and an especially feminine demeanor. Whenever she looked at me, I felt as though she was trying to decide whether or not she should like me. There seemed to be some criteria of which I was unaware. Smiling, she waved as Hank and I rounded the corner and continued our tour.

In the little office next to Elaine's space sat Mike Bling, Hank's partner. Although southern born and bred, he spoke so quickly his words ran together. Although he was a young-looking thirty-five, his manufactured cowlick in front of his buzz cut was noticeably out of place.

Mentally focused on deciphering the polite gibberish Mike was machine-gunning in my direction, I still managed to catch only a small portion of what he said. I walked out the door sensing I had just met Alex P. Keaton from the 1980s sitcom *Family Ties*. It was to be my most accurate assessment of the day.

In the corner opposite Hank was the office of Mr. Ted Tiller, senior vice president of investments. As we approached his office, the open door allowed me a glimpse of a balding man leaning over a desk drawer that contained several rows of coins, which he was busily counting and organizing.

As we walked into his office, the contrast to everyone else's space was striking. There was no paper anywhere. His desk was not only uncluttered, it was uninhabited. A distinguished looking gentleman of about fifty-five, Ted stood to shake my hand. He was not as thick as Rudy Mantooth, but at six feet six inches, Ted was nonetheless a large man.

Any native South Carolinian would have immediately recognized this man's accent. It was South of Broad all right, no doubt about it—right here in Blueberg, some three hundred miles inland. The blueblood pecking order, which is important to understand as a financial advisor in our state, begins south of

Broad Street in Charleston, South Carolina. These bluebloods are defined by those whose families originated from homes located in the battery area of the old city commonly referred to as South of Broad. No blood in America is any bluer than corpuscles from south of Broad Street in Charleston.

I was later to learn Ted's accent was somewhat tainted. He had acquired it from his days at a prep school in Charleston. His family was actually from Columbia.

After our introductions, Tiller sat back down in his high-backed office chair, his eyes swiftly focusing again on his coinage.

Just outside Ted Tiller's office was the office of his teammate, Sam Reagan. Sam was to become my best friend at Merrill Lynch. I was forty-five, and he was forty-three. He had actually read a book or two, which gave me more in common with him than with the other advisors. After practicing estate planning and tax law, Sam had been lured away from the law firm next door to Merrill Lynch to provide assistance to Ted—a much bigger job than it appeared my first time around the horn.

I came to work for Merrill Lynch Blueberg just prior to the renovation that was promised Rudy and Richard upon their departure from Smith Barney. During the renovation, Ted encroached six inches into Sam's office space to ensure that his was still the largest Merrill Lynch office in Blueberg.

The up-fit on the other side of the office to accommodate Rudy and Richard had enlarged Hank's office ever so slightly due to a ventilation issue, and to make things right, Ted had grabbed six long inches of Sam's precious space. All of this made no difference to Sam whatsoever, but it appeared to be the most important thing in Ted's life until everything was ironed out and the plans had been approved by corporate.

Sam had been sucked into the promise of a blueblood partner in a blueblood business, which made the money look good, very good, at the time he made his decision to give up the legal profession. Having grown up in Blueberg, Sam knew Ted's reputation and had seen all of the accoutrements of affluence Ted so skillfully displayed in his life. He was therefore susceptible to the meticulous ruse that was Ted Tiller.

Next in the office lineup was Reggie Sparks. Reggie had been the high school quarterback in a small town just north of Blueberg. At thirty-five years of age, he probably could have still taken the hit on a quarterback sneak. He had gray matter not usually associated with a jock. Well groomed, he looked younger than his age, but when he spoke his words were measured, which added an unexpected maturity to his conversation.

Boyishly handsome, Reggie had married Bridgette, a striking blond personal trainer. In a move to test his wealth management industry mettle, Reggie had threatened to leave the firm if Merrill Lynch had no place for him on a team of financial advisors. The firm acquiesced and paired him with an advisor nearing retirement.

It was a smart move by Merrill and a home run for Reggie. All he had to do was show up and make no grievous errors. If he could endure for five years, he was sure to pocket around $400,000 per year. In Blueberg, South Carolina, that's real money. Only two things could derail the train: greed and/or a horrific financial crisis.

Diagonally in the offices on the other side of the bullpen sat the old pros. As I was introduced to them, I could tell these guys were industry veterans. Down to earth and sincere, Bill Mitchell and Harley Johnson were friendly and easy to speak with. They both had worked at the company for twenty years and had offices next to each other. As I tried to evaluate the people I was meeting on the fly (with little success, I might add), with so many similarities I found myself assigning them to the same mental file folder.

In an entirely different section of the office, Herb Camp occupied the office against the far back wall next to the supply closet. Herb's father had been my father's boss for an extended period when both worked for Big Red Textiles. Being much older than my dad, Mr. Camp had retired some twenty years before my father, but still it was another connection for me in the office.

Herb had a slight recollection of me as a child, which made for a good, comfortable conversation that first day. He was about my height but much rounder. A former high school athlete, Herb was a sports junkie. His life revolved around watching sporting events, forming an opinion about each play, and then sharing it with as many people as humanly possible. His office looked like a tornado had just passed through. There was a reason Herb was in the back.

The end of my tour brought Hank and me back to the cube that was to be my home. Waiting for us was Lucy Stone, who had been with the firm over twenty years. Lucy was to be my assistant and my go-to person in the office. Her job was to answer my questions and guide me. Somewhere north of fifty years old, Lucy had red hair and carried the smell of cigarette smoke. Although attractive for her age, my guess was that in her day Lucy Stone was a babelicious chick with an attitude. She was the nervous type and not able to deal with stress smoothly, but she was quick to recover from just about any situation.

Lucy was recognized as having the most technology know-how of anyone in the office, which made it readily apparent that the most basic concepts of computing were far beyond where any of my coworkers ever dared venture. I may have been at the bottom of the financial industry's learning curve, but when it came to understanding the piece of technology on my desk, I was already far ahead of Lucy and everyone else in that office. I was uncertain about a lot of things, but one thing was clear: to be successful in this business, an ability to utilize the Merrill Lynch software was not a prerequisite.

Lucy was to help me sign on to the Merrill Lynch computer network and create my personage in the cyberspace known as the Merrill Lynch Wealth Management workstation. Having my ml.com e-mail address and a workstation ID "created" me at Merrill Lynch.

After a couple of days, Lucy finally was able to get me signed on. Since I was the first financial advisor to be hired in three years, the procedures had changed and Lucy had to learn them. During my first four days with the company, I sat in my cube and read a book so Scott Hotham could enjoy his bonus.

Lucy also worked with Herb Camp and Bill Mitchell. She made it plain from the start that Bill's needs came first. After all, he was a million-dollar revenue producer, the crème de la crème at Merrill Lynch. Within the first three days, Lucy painted for me her interpretation of the situation. She explained how many aspiring financial advisors like me she had seen come and go in her time, clearly delivering her message: don't cause me problems, and I'll get around to your needs at my convenience.

She was straightforward, and I appreciated that. I also understood that she was shaping the dynamics of our relationship, which was the sure sign of a veteran of office politics. For the moment I had no choice but to play along and submit. The fish I aimed to fry at Merrill Lynch were larger than winning the ego game with Lucy.

I tried to let my sense of humor carry the day and felt successful most of the time. People in Lucy's position can either help or hurt you, and I am proud to say that over the course of my time at Merrill Lynch she and I became friends. I learned to respect her on several different levels, and I think she trusted me as much as anyone in the office.

2. Pledging the Fraternity

These mist covered mountains
Are a home now for me.
But my home is the lowlands
And always will be.
Some day you'll return to
Your valleys and your farms
And you'll no longer burn
To be brothers in arms.

—**Mark Knopfler**

A t Merrill Lynch, every financial advisor candidate has one initial purpose in life: to pass the Series 7 exam. To that end, I began to study the online material provided by Merrill Lynch. It was a deluge of information. To break the strain of learning so much new information, I was also asked to develop a business plan in my spare time. As I contemplated how I might form a beachhead in the wealth management marketplace invasion I was planning, my little hometown of Folksy seemed like the perfect Normandy.

One week after my debut in the financial services industry, my plan fell apart.

It began over at Smith Barney Blueberg, where Dick Plum, the office manager, always took his annual fishing trip to Canada during the first week of

August. (The timing of Rudy and Richard's departure a year earlier from Smith Barney had coincided with Plum's broadcasted vulnerability.) Sure enough, subterfuge was in the air. At Merrill Lynch, the office next to Reggie Sparks, which I thought would be mine soon, was mysteriously cleaned out. The office atmosphere was highly charged, and Hassy Meadows could not hide her excitement about something. Late Friday afternoon, just hours after Dick Plum boarded the plane on his way to the tundra, another of Hank Patton's espionage operations sprang to fruition.

Smith Barney financial advisors Emily Smith and her uncle, Tom Hawkins, walked in the front door at our Merrill Lynch office and supplanted me as the newest additions to the advisor corps.

The office erupted in congratulatory celebration. I wasn't too happy. Tom Hawkins and I go way back, having both grown up in Folksy. My business plan had consisted of a strategy to reach the moneyed gentry in that town. His clients were the ones I had planned on capturing for the home team.

Tom didn't seem too happy either, but my presence had nothing to do with it. He had been with Smith Barney for thirty years, and he looked a little shell-shocked as the excitement came to a crescendo. Emily Smith, on the other hand, was ecstatic. A slender woman of thirty-five, suggestively dressed, she was taking in the glory.

As the new advisors stood around the bullpen describing the play-by-play of their exodus, the degree of planning and execution of their move took me aback. The glee of envisioning Dick Plum's face as he received the news that for the second consecutive year two of his income machines had jumped ship during his fishing trip only sweetened the conquest for Hank, Rudy, Richard, and Emily. Tom seemed to have a melancholy outlook on the situation. I didn't quite grasp the significance of the moment. If Tom and Emily wanted to change jobs, what was the big deal? Boy, was I naïve.

This late Friday afternoon gathering was soon invaded by a party of ten or so commandos from the complex headquarters in Charlotte. At about four thirty, this team of young thirtysomethings, wearing blue jeans and T-shirts (that's what made them commandos), swooped in carrying boxes of forms, computer lists, and envelopes. The cavalry had ridden in—or the transition team, as it were—right on time.

In addition to being paid between two and three times their annual commissions in bonus money, Tom and Emily had been promised logistical help moving their accounts from Smith Barney to Merrill Lynch. My guess is that each probably received $500,000, with $250,000 in cash and the remainder paid in Merrill Lynch stock restricted for the length of the agreement, which was probably five years. It is tradition to hand the checks to the recruited FAs as they walk in the door on the day of days, and I'm sure this Friday was the most lucrative day either Emily or Tom had ever experienced.

The procedure was well choreographed, and I sat shocked and awed at the manpower Merrill Lynch so swiftly brought to bear on the situation. It was a humbling display of raw corporate power. Commandeering our conference room, the transition team was obviously preparing for an all-nighter as an assembly line of paperwork topped the long conference room table, and pizzas were ordered as a matter of course.

The bare-knuckles brawl with Smith Barney over the Hawkins and Smith team's accounts was well under way. Everyone involved knew that two blocks up the street in the Smith Barney office, the alarm had been sounded, and the enemy was surely marshalling their forces for a counterattack. From their weekend retreats, all the Smith Barney FAs were summoned for the development of stratagem that would convince the clients in play to stay at Smith Barney with them as their new advisors.

At that very moment, Tom and Emily's clients were being divided among their former colleagues as the spoils of an FA defection (called a "book distribution," in trade jargon). This was an event FAs lived for. Soon Emily and Tom's clients would be under siege. The new additions to the Merrill Lynch team had to frantically get signatures on the transfer paperwork while the Smith Barney advisors would be attempting to thwart their efforts. The Smith Barney advisors would be urging caution and pleading for consideration to forestall the signing of any paperwork. Since the time frame was short and the payoff large, this was a situation that often dissolved into a contest of dirty tricks.

Of course the largest accounts were being contacted immediately. I am sure the majority of those clients had no idea it was possible for their personal financial information to be shared among all the brokers at Smith Barney, but that is what happens in a book distribution. In this frenzy of greed, time is of the essence, and rules are made to be bent. The carcass of Emily and Tom's clients was on the ground, and the scavengers were intensely focused on dragging it up into their tree. This was blood sport of the first order. Game on.

Prior to 2004, financial services firms were constantly embroiled in lawsuits as a result of broker migrations to competing firms. The courts became more and more concerned that the public interest was not being served due to clauses in the industry's standard non-compete agreements that effectively precluded clients of the migrating broker from selecting the financial advisor of their choice.

In 2004, Smith Barney, Merrill Lynch, and UBS Financial Services entered into the Protocol for Broker Recruiting agreement. This agreement set a protocol for operations such as the one Hank Patton had conducted, first with Richard and Rudy, and now with Emily and Tom. According to the protocol, only certain information could be carried by the migrating broker: name, address, and telephone number. No financial information such as account numbers and balances were allowed. The one rule that stood above all others, the rule that could not be broken, was the notification or discussion with clients of an impending move.

Breaking this rule meant the protocol was no longer applicable, and the lawsuits would start to fly. The stakes were too large, the stream of income too great. These amounts of money warranted the most expensive legal actions, and the offended firm would surely act to protect its interest.

Even though Tom's arrival forced me to scrap my business plan, I was glad he was in the office. Tom had worked for my father and Herb Camp's father at Big Red Textiles, a Folksy manufacturer, some thirty-five years ago. Tom knew my family well, and he actually had taken my bird dog when I went away to college. Although both of us were teetotalers, Tom and I had bent many an elbow together years ago. Pushing sixty-five, Tom was still working and as sharp as ever. Overall, having him in the office was a plus for me.

Days later, as excitement over the new wealth management landscape in Blueberg faded, my daily conquest of the Series 7 material began in earnest. Being as friendly as possible and wanting badly to fit into the body politic, I was closely tuned in to the everyday conversation of the office. But toward the end of my second week, I noticed something odd: whenever I came into the room, the chatter over the cube walls subsided.

One day, after about two weeks of eerie quiet, Susan Sanders, the small, attractive lady who sat in the cubical behind me, whispered over the divider, "I can't wait until we can talk to you." This brought on my first moment of clarity at Merrill Lynch. My isolation was being orchestrated. People have a motive for everything they do, so I sat staring at my computer screen, wondering what effect this isolation was supposed to produce in me.

As the only trainee in the Blueberg office, I traveled to the Pleasantburg office each Tuesday to meet with others of my ilk. It was there I first heard the term "Merrillized." The isolation was a part of my Merrillization. Knowing this helped me deal with the daily oddities more effectively by openly asking how my Merrillization was coming in the opinion of Management ("Management" was Hank's office nickname).

The closest analogy to Merrillization I can think of is the indoctrination associated with joining a college fraternity. After the spell of isolation was over, I entered into what I call the pledge phase of my Merrillization. Not being a fraternity brother in my college days, I had trouble relating to the pledge designation.

Almost daily, mutual fund or annuity wholesalers would take all the FAs in the office to lunch. "Pledges" who had no business to offer in exchange for lunch were affectionately known as "plate lickers."

The other financial advisors loved giving me a hard time about my station in life because they knew I could take it. I also knew that had they not liked me on some level, the isolation would have continued or morphed into some form of malignant tolerance. I tried to take the good with the bad, but I could see that the process was a use of fear and intimidation to control behavior and to make sure new hires were properly indoctrinated into the culture.

If I had known about this aspect of the industry, I might have been able to negotiate around my time in the cube. This effort to play mind games seemed ridiculous to me and certainly had a negative effect on my productivity. As the people from Folksy would put it, "I never have threatened real good." I had spent the better part of my life trying to make decisions and conduct my affairs free of fear. The aura of arrogance in this culture should have clued me in to the coming conflicts, but I remained naïve to the ramifications of such a self-righteous attitude. Through years of practice, the industry management had cleverly disguised the true nature of the forces lurking just below the organization's surface.

After the excitement of Emily and Tom's arrival began to wane, the office was thrown into turmoil by the construction project promised Richard and Rudy. Due to Ted's six-inch expansion requirement, the plans had taken over a year to be approved. Once construction started, the entire office fell into a makeshift order to accommodate the intrusion of contractors. FAs make their living on the telephone, and noisy contractors do nothing but subtract from productivity.

I was moved out of my cube, but it was my good fortune to land in the large conference room between Richard and Hassy. Sitting next to Richard was a learning experience I could not have purchased. Having been in the business for twenty-two years, Richard had developed a shtick honed to perfection, first at Smith Barney and now at Merrill Lynch.

Born into one of South Carolina's wealthiest families, Richard had a grandfather who was one of the original investment bankers on Wall Street. As an adolescent, during visits to his grandparents' home in old Virginia, Richard had at his disposal a chauffeur to ferry him about town. Although Hank Patton and Ted Tiller were from families with old and substantial wealth, they were not in Richard's league. The education I received sitting next to him had little to do with the intricacies of the financial services industry.

The value Richard placed on himself to the exclusion of all others was obvious, blatant, and downright shocking. So much so that it was the vulnerability used to needle him when the office barbs began to fly (this and the childhood chauffeur, a piece of information I am sure he regrets sharing).

The renovation interruption lasted for an excruciating two months, after which I was placed back in my cube while Richard and Rudy were enthroned in their new office complete with a conference room table. To outsiders, this may seem a small detail, but in the establishment of a pecking order, Richard and Rudy knew the importance of how things looked to everyone else in the office.

The first situation that foreshadowed my future conflict with Merrill Lynch occurred right after Richard and Rudy moved into their new digs, about nine months into my employment. Unlike the Merrillization issue, this threat of trouble to come did not escape my recognition.

Every two years, a ritual known as "insurance continuing education" is inflicted on South Carolinians holding insurance licenses. To sell annuities and long-term care insurance in the state, financial advisors are required to hold a life and health insurance license. The dreaded requirement in South Carolina is twenty-four classroom hours of instruction pertaining to exciting topics including annuities, life insurance concepts, and long-term care innovations. As a former insurance agency owner, I was accustomed to serving my time. But at Merrill Lynch, things are handled differently.

Since the requirement had an impending deadline, Ted Tiller announced that our instructor would be in our office the following Monday. I thought it very strange that the appointment was at four thirty. The instructor, Bruce Nickerson, arrived at the appointed time, and all of the FAs were called into Rudy and Richard's new office.

As we entered the room, Ted Tiller informed us that for the meager sum of $187, Bruce was going to provide our continuing education requirement. At this point I was still under the impression that class would begin the following morning. Ted asked everyone to pull out their checkbooks and write Bruce a check. Much to my surprise, Bruce began circulating a roll verification document we were to sign, stating we had been in a continuing education class all day that day.

Coming from the insurance industry, I was stunned at the bold fraud being committed. I could see that closely following the first document was a second indicating we had been in class all day the following day.

Immediately I knew I had to make an escape. Luckily my cell phone was in my pocket, providing the perfect opportunity to fake a call requiring my urgent attention. I left the room and walked to my car, all the while pretending to talk on the phone. As I drove away, my phone really did ring. It was my friend Sam Reagan, asking what time I would return to the office.

I told Sam, a former attorney, that in my opinion fraud was being committed regarding the continuing education requirement and I could not participate. I could hear the angst in his voice, and instead of discussing the matter, I told him to tell Hank that I would take an online course.

This event really disturbed me and caused me to ask some hard questions, but time smoothed them over as I fell back into the Merrill Lynch daily routine.

I was making a sixty-mile commute each day, and to avoid traffic I would leave home around six thirty in the morning, which meant most mornings I was the first to arrive at the office, usually right before eight o'clock. Often my arrival coincided with Sam's. We became good friends, sharing those first cups of coffee in the morning.

Sam Reagan was an ethical, stand-up sort of guy. He understood the paradoxical nature of the Bible, and we had read many of the same books, but nonetheless it was awkward to speak with him about the continuing education issue. To the rest of the financial advisors it was a minor detail, but to me, a former insurance agent, continuing education was no trifling matter.

As I had feared, my phony phone call had fooled no one. It was obvious I was not going to play ball on this, and Sam expressed to me that I was taking an unnecessary risk by making too big a deal out of something that was immaterial. There was a part of Sam that was very secretive, and I knew he was not telling me all he knew. Heretofore my assimilation into the office culture had been going smashingly. The acceptance of my station as a pledge had indicated to the other financial advisors I knew my place and the rules of the pecking order. But my exhibiting independence and demonstrating unwillingness to blindly follow the herd had taken many in the office by surprise.

I had expected as much and decided to let the matter drop, with one caveat. I went to Hank Patton and explained the reason for my actions. The matter was seemingly forgotten, and there was no price to be paid for my revolt. My Merrillization, as far as management was concerned, continued on track.

Having achieved a passing score on the Series 7, the wealth management candidate is qualified to take the Series 66 exam. While the Series 7 exam is crammed full of investment facts and relationships, the Series 66 exam tests the candidate's legal knowledge. I thought the Series 7 was slightly more difficult.

Passing both exams and earning a license to dispense financial advice is a milestone in the early career of any FA, but it pales in comparison to graduation from the "Paths of Achievement" training program when the place you work is Merrill Lynch.

Once licensed, the FA qualifies for a production number. This is not just any number; it is THE number. Advisors are persona non grata in the financial services industry until a number is bestowed by the sponsoring firm. Giving an FA a number is like christening a ship. It designates a person as a source of income within the firm.

At Merrill Lynch, once a production number is assigned to a financial advisor, the quest for real legitimacy begins. Production of income is closely monitored; the days of being a plate licker are numbered, one way or the other.

Achieving these milestones meant I was also now qualified for a Merrill Lynch business card. Merrill Lynch doesn't allow plate lickers to carry the Bull around on a business card. It was part of the psychological Stockholm syndrome game the firm plays with pledges as part of the Merrillization process. For six months I had toiled at Merrill Lynch without being able to give anyone a business card with my office telephone number on it.

3. Fifteen-Million-Dollar Mountain

Great expectations, everybody's watching you.
People you meet, they all seem to know you.
Even your old friends treat you like you're something new.

– Don Henley, Glenn Fry, and J. D. Souther

After passing the examinations and obtaining a license and production number, the rookie financial advisor is up to bat in the most crucial period any aspiring FA must survive. And make no mistake—survival is what it's all about.

The goal is, by some hook or crook, to graduate the training program. To do this, the advisor must pass two courses, pass two evaluations conducted by the Path of Achievement (POA) coach, and, above all, accumulate $15 million in assets to manage.

I had no trouble passing the courses, and Paul Presley, my POA coach in Pleasantburg, said there was no need for the evaluations since Hank had given me the thumbs-up. He added that as far as he was concerned, I knew enough to sell, and being a second-career guy, he believed I was mature enough to manage my business.

Indeed, I was mature enough to manage my business, but this was the first overt indication I'd received that success wasn't about getting it *right*, it was about getting it *sold*. There is a world of difference between the two, and it was becoming more and more apparent which one Merrill Lynch—and by extension, the financial services industry—valued the most.

The first two requirements for POA graduation were simply motions to go through, but that last criterion was a horse of a different color. Gathering $15 million in assets was a tall order. It was a tall order in the much larger city of Pleasantburg, or even in Atlanta for that matter, but putting together $15 million in Blueberg seemed damn near impossible. Frankly, I really did not understand how anyone could pull it off, but if anyone could, I felt like I was the man.

The more I studied how little new production the experienced FAs were doing, the steeper the $15 million hill became in my mind. When I asked about the probabilities of success in Blueberg given the level of production our most capable FAs were squeaking out, management's explanation was that since my time was unencumbered by existing accounts, I should be much more effective bringing in new accounts than my more experienced colleagues.

Theoretically, a smart and gifted new producer with a singular focus on account acquisition could yield fabulous results. Since I was the first rookie FA hired at Blueberg in six years (Sam had been hired three years ago, but since he had a law degree and was brought in specifically to babysit Ted, he was never in the POA training program), no examples or role models were readily available. In any case, since no one had blazed the trail ahead to show me how it was done, time spent bemoaning the fact was time wasted. There was nothing left to do but follow the hallowed advice of that internationally recognized intellectual, Larry the Cable Guy, and "get 'er done."

The reason my trail had not been blazed is that two years before I was hired by Merrill Lynch, the wealth management world was set on its ear. The profound change was an unintended consequence when the national do-not-call list was implemented. The Federal Trade Commission had responded to the call (no pun intended) of the masses who were fed up with being interrupted by telemarketers every night as they sat down to the dinner table. Putting your name on the do-not-call list brought these interruptions to a screeching halt.

In the past, successful financial advisors were essentially members of one of two groups. The first group consisted of advisors birthed into wealthy families. In the trade it is known as coming down the right chute. The second group consisted of those with an innate ability to dial for dollars. Dialing for dollars involved buying a six-pack of beer, going to the office, and calling as many prospective clients as humanly possible before nine o'clock at night. The second group relied solely on the law of large numbers. In other words, if you throw enough mud against the wall, some of it is bound to stick.

I did not come down the right chute, and under the new rules, I couldn't throw enough mud against the wall. My challenge to succeed in this new environment was going to require some thought, some strategy, and a whole lot of luck. I had to believe that if I worked hard, learned voraciously, and treated my clients as I would want to be treated, Merrill Lynch would provide a path to success. There had to be a way to succeed, or Merrill Lynch would not be investing money in my training. So I set out to find the magic formula.

I knew from running organizations that a valued employee would be guided down the right road. When comparing my skill set to my office colleagues, there was never any question in my mind that one way or another I would earn a seat at the table. Surely Merrill Lynch management was putting the trainees through a vetting process and would make every effort to retain deserving candidates. With a look on his face that left no doubt he knew something I didn't, Hank constantly encouraged me by saying, "Keep doing what you're doing, and everything will be fine." As comforting as his words were, the whole progression was a little unnerving, just as I later learned it was designed to be.

A new financial advisor at Merrill Lynch is assigned a senior FA with whom to share a production number until the newcomer graduates from the training program. As a means of motivating and rewarding trainees, Merrill Lynch had a time-sensitive bonus system in place. Reach the $15 million goal in twelve months, and the hardy producer earns a $100,000 bonus: $50,000 in cash and $50,000 in Merrill Lynch restricted stock (stock that the new hire would not own until after ten years with the firm, a fact they failed to explain in my interview).

As each three-month period passes, the bonus is whittled away by a certain amount. If the entire allotted twenty-four months is used, the pot of gold is only $5,000. At that point the advisor is just worried about keeping his or her job, and the $5,000 means very little. I am doubtful that very many of these situations occurred. Such candidates are long gone before the twenty-four months is up. In order to spur the advisor on, small bonuses were also paid for achieving milestones that indicated sufficient progress toward the ultimate goal. These amounts were around $2,500. To help me down this path, Bill Mitchell was made my mentor.

As a producer who generated over $1 million in revenue for the firm, Bill was accommodated whenever possible around the Blueberg Office. He was a likable man, active in his church, and extremely conscientious regarding his responsibilities. He and I both started our careers in the insurance business.

While I sold business insurance, he was a claims adjuster. Bill had the personality of a claims adjuster— extremely frugal and attentive to detail.

I admired Bill for many reasons but primarily for his aversion to office politics. Although he was to guide me, he really had no idea of the issues I faced. He had been successful as a financial advisor by being honest, hardworking (making a lot of cold calls), and always being around at book distribution time.

Bill was always busy. Through twenty-one years of service at Merrill Lynch, he had accumulated a massive pile of small- to medium-sized accounts. In addition to the number of accounts Bill had, his demographic was also labor-intensive. Somehow he had gravitated to the octogenarian market. Little old ladies loved Bill. To say his book of accounts was aged would be an understatement. It seemed he and Lucy had a client die almost every month—sometimes two or three a month.

Any question I had was necessarily squeezed between Bill's life quest of fulfilling his obligation to each client. Although he was being compensated (meagerly) to be my mentor and would have inherited certain accounts in the event of my early departure, I felt as though any question was an imposition on his time. Still, he was helpful, and he came through for me in a big way when it counted.

In the spring of 2007, I was grinding away at the momentous $15 million requirement, making slow progress. Within the next three months, two important events changed my life at Merrill Lynch. The first was a move from the cube into a supply closet that I was permitted to convert into an office. I even had to bring my own desk from home, but it was worth every bit of the hassle.

The second event was the key that unlocked the gate to the yellow brick road that led to my accumulation of $15 million in assets and graduation from the POA training program.

Early that spring I was called into Hank Patton's office, given a list of names, and told these clients were now my responsibility. By far this was the best news I had received since joining the firm. Scanning the list of these forty-five or so names, my eyes were drawn to the column labeled total assets. The column's sum held a number in the neighborhood of $2.5 million. Hank made a point of informing me that his generosity was only made possible by the cooperation of Mike Bling, his partner.

I was overwhelmed with gratitude and a sense of responsibility to the names on that list. Walking back to my tiny office, I felt I held the roadmap to $15 million in assets in my hands. The fog had lifted. It was clear that if I continued working diligently, fitting into the office culture, and making no problems up the managerial chain, Hank had the ability to secure me a position as a financial advisor with Merrill Lynch. I was encouraged, enlightened, and enthusiastic about my future prospects in the wealth management business.

What I did not understand was that these accounts held *dead assets*. At the time it made no difference to me because the $2.5 million counted toward my $15 million goal. The accounts held two types of investments with some variety mixed in: cash, individual stocks, and other investments that paid little or no income. Financial advisors do not earn commission on cash, nor do they earn commission on individual stocks unless they are traded—ergo the term "dead assets."

The stocks in these accounts were not being traded. These accounts were being held by Hank and Mike as an extension of their power base. Having the ability to dole them out, Hank and Mike were the office kingmakers, or financial-advisor-makers, as it were. It seemed to me an ingenious method of vetting candidates, ensuring that only those meeting their approval would be around for long. I felt honored by their confidence and benevolence. I worked all the harder and felt an intense loyalty to Hank.

Earlier in the spring, I had proved my mettle by securing $2 million in assets from my first prospective client seminar. Sam had agreed to help me with the seminar, which was held some seventy-five miles from our office. The thing I remember most about that seminar was the question Sam asked as we discussed our presentation plan during the drive to the country club. "Who are we going to be today: New York Wall Streeters or good old boys from the down-home South?"

The question had stunned me. I replied, "Let's just be Sam and Hal and see how things go." Although his objection was unspoken, I could tell Sam had no confidence in that plan. Gaining two accounts at $1 million each vindicated my approach. Hank and the others in the office were shocked yet excited by my success. I am sure Hank and Mike would not have been so forthcoming with the dead assets had I not demonstrated some prior ability.

The seminar experience reinforced my belief that regardless of what I might be expected to do, being honest and straightforward in this new endeavor would lead to long-term success. After the seminar, I was sure I could maintain my ethical standards in this industry, although I realized it was going to take an effort of conscience and eternal vigilance.

4. Put Me In, Coach

Put me in, coach
I'm ready to play
Today
Look at me
I can be
Centerfield

– John Fogerty

R arely in life do dreams come true and turn out as well as the dream itself. In the early fall of 2006, I personally had a dream come true in a most unique fashion, and it turned out to benefit me both personally and professionally.

Anyone who has lived in South Carolina for long knows the importance of college football to the state's culture. In South Carolina's football-crazy tradition, coaches and players at the rival schools of Clemson University and the University of South Carolina become heroes and legends. As a lifelong, die-hard Clemson fan, I was privileged to attend church with one of those legends. Former Clemson head football coach Danny Ford and his wife Deborah were regular attendees of Clemson Presbyterian Church, and I had the pleasure of teaching a Sunday school class Deborah attended regularly. My wife Anita and I had actually been out to the Ford's house for dinner one evening. This was one of the great perks associated with living in Tigertown.

As a young man, I had traveled to Miami on New Year's night in 1982 to watch thirty-one-year-old Danny Ford lead his Tiger football team to victory over the Nebraska Cornhuskers, claiming the national championship for Clemson University. For someone who had grown up watching the Tigers play, from my seat underneath the oak tree that used to grow where the band now sits on the famed "Hill" in Death Valley, it was a night of nirvana in south Florida. The young coach who was hoisted onto the shoulders of his players and carried off the field that night became the hero of Tiger Nation forever.

After leaving Clemson and a brief stint at the University of Arkansas, Coach Ford had retired back to his farm in a little town right outside of Clemson. With his name on the side of the stadium and a respect that only South Carolina football fans can endow, Coach Ford is truly a living legend. Having him as one of my clients at Merrill Lynch would be singularly the best accomplishment I could conceive of at that early point in my career.

As luck would have it, Coach Ford was scheduled to speak at the Blueberg Touchdown Club prior to Clemson's annual game against the Florida State Seminoles. Since I was commuting from Clemson to Blueberg, I offered to give him a ride. To my delight, he accepted.

As we drove to Blueberg, the conversation naturally turned to investments. Carefully I threw out a couple of opinions and what their implications might be. At the end of the ride, Coach Ford agreed to continue the conversation the following week.

The outcome of this serendipitous opportunity was more than I could have hoped for. In anticipation of the next meeting, I decided to compensate for my inexperience by inviting Rudy and Richard to accompany me on this all-important appointment. I called Coach Ford, mentioned my colleagues, and Coach graciously invited us out to his farm.

On the appointed day, Rudy, Richard, and I pulled up to the barn where the coach was vaccinating his calves. As we stepped out of the car in our Sunday-go-to-meetin' clothes, I noticed the coach was dressed in a muddy T-shirt and an even muddier pair of jeans. We watched as he chased a young calf down a chute closed off by a gate. As the calf approached the gate, Coach would pull the gate back, trapping the calf between the gate and fence. Once the calf was corralled, the coach would grab a syringe he carried between his teeth and inject his patient with the medicine. Seeing us approach, he turned his latest victim loose into the pasture and came over to shake our hands.

In less than two minutes, Richard had made a determination. He said, "Coach, you need to sell everything you have and then buy gold and oil." So much for carefully understanding the client's risk profile, goals, and current circumstances before making a diversified investment portfolio recommendation.

Unflappable as always, Coach (most people call him Danny, but to me he will always be Coach) asked a few questions about some oil stocks while silently gauging Richard and Rudy's credibility. After some polite conversation, Coach went back to the job at hand.

Not really knowing what else to do, I hung my jacket on the fence post, rolled up my sleeves, and manned the gate. As Richard and Rudy regaled Coach Ford with a detailed analysis of the S&P 500 and shared profound market predictions, I pressed the gate against the calves as Coach Ford administered the inoculations.

Once the job was done, Richard, Rudy, and I got in the car and headed back to Blueberg. Richard and Rudy seemed happy. Regardless of whether or not Coach Ford let us manage a nickel, they'd had a chance to see the man alive and in action, true to his persona.

Danny Ford is an interesting man with rare qualities. He has nothing to prove to anyone, a trait that gives him the unique ability to shoot straight, be honest, and to wear an authenticity seldom found in celebrity. He is proud of his Alabama roots, and his homespun outlook fits nicely on his sleeve. There are many stories of sophisticates who have misinterpreted this genuineness for a lack of intelligence, much to their detriment. They seem to allow his manner to obscure his résumé. I learned a lot from watching and listening to Danny Ford. A unique ability to sift through situations and target the real issues is truly one of Coach Ford's greatest gifts. I can easily see how he recruited great athletes to schools where he coached.

Danny Ford played for legendary coach Bear Bryant at Alabama, where he was all-conference academically as well as athletically. He holds both an undergraduate and a master's degree. At age thirty-one, he took Clemson football to the pinnacle of the college football world by winning the 1981 national championship, the youngest coach ever to do so.

All those accomplishments are in the public record. What's not part of the public record are all the things he does behind the scenes. Trying to figure out a convenient time to meet was sometimes difficult. Coach Ford had to go sign some balls for this boy, or call a pastor on his birthday because his father was ill, or go to see someone in the hospital—all things he did because he wanted to and never considered living his life any other way. Nobody sees all he does for his friends, neighbors, and even complete strangers because he genuinely cares about people. Danny Ford is no lightweight by anyone's measure.

Three days after our meeting at the farm, I called Coach for some feedback. He never mentioned Richard and Rudy, so neither did I. He told me to come over. He had some money to invest with me. Even though the amount was small, this was one of the best days of my life. For the trust he had placed in me, Coach Ford was going to receive service beyond his expectations and an undying loyalty. Nobody was going to shortchange Danny Ford on my watch.

Whenever Coach Ford dropped by the Merrill Lynch office, it was an event. His easy nature and sense of humor made everyone glad to see him.

Everyone except me. Coach Ford is a hard man to work for, and sometimes that straightforwardness I respected made for a good case of heartburn. He would ask me the same question three different ways to see if I would give him the same answer.

I learned early on that he never forgot anything you told him about his money. I also learned that if I made a mistake, it was better to own up right away. It didn't keep him from chewing you out, but he did it with respect. As hard as it was to tell him bad news, I vowed to never shade the facts with half-truths, a huge temptation in the wealth management profession. It was not an easy road to take, but the policy paid enormous dividends down the road.

My first chance to be of service to Coach involved two different investment opportunities he was considering. He was buying a bull one day near Blueberg and asked me to meet him. He had two proposals from companies out in Texas that he wanted me to evaluate. The management teams were to be in Pleasantburg, and he wanted me to come hear the pitch. After taking everything in and based on some research I did before the meeting, I knew these guys were desperately trying to raise cash. Why would a legitimate oil and gas outfit from Texas need money from South Carolina? A quick review of the numbers confirmed my suspicions, and I shared my thoughts with Coach, with the preface that I was unqualified to give an official opinion. I turned out to be right, and the coach did not forget it.

In early December of 2006, I would receive a call that would again send my career at Merrill Lynch in a new direction. Sitting in my office mulling over the holidays and how I might conquer the $15 million beast clawing at my door, I heard the phone ring. On the other end was Bradley Kannup, the biggest producer in South Carolina, calling from the Merrill Lynch office in Columbia.

"Hal," he said, "I just got word from Arkansas that Danny Ford's Merrill Lynch advisor has left the firm for Morgan Stanley. I called Danny to see if my team here in Columbia could help." (Having this type of intelligence went a long way in explaining why his was the largest team in South Carolina.) "He said that he already has a relationship with you and wants you to handle his account."

The implications of this statement washed over me. The meager sum I had accepted from Coach and my later good advice to him were now paying off. I called and asked Coach Ford if we could meet for dinner in Pleasantburg, and he readily agreed.

This was big. I went to Hank to ask if he and Don Plaus, the regional director, could go with me to the meeting. Given Coach's celebrity and the size of his account, they immediately accepted my invitation.

We made reservations at the best restaurant in Pleasantburg and requested a private room. I quickly learned that you never tried to conduct business with Coach anytime the public had access to him. He attracted rock-star-like crowds and endless requests for his autograph. It was impossible to have a meaningful dialogue in a public setting, although it was fun to watch.

In stark contrast to Richard and Rudy, the finesse of Don and Hank went beyond my expectations. I have been to several rodeos in my professional career, and Don Plaus is hands-down the best I have ever seen in front of the client. At the end of the meeting, Coach agreed to move his account to South Carolina. Such was the origin of an odyssey I could never have imagined.

5. The Politics of Fear

Money, get away
Get a good job with more pay, and you're okay.
Money, it's a gas
Grab that cash with both hands and make a stash.

– Roger Waters

My relationship with Coach Ford provided me with credibility in the office that would not have been possible otherwise. Not only did it demonstrate my abilities, but it was a source of pride for everyone in the office. The account let everyone in the office know that I was not, and never had been, a pledge, and that maybe there was some measure of potential for me in the business. This was an important component of the auditioning process to secure a position on a team of advisors. A team offered revenue-sharing opportunities, greater bonuses, and more negotiating leverage with management. By pooling resources, teams of advisors are oftentimes greater than the sum of their parts. This creates stability and longevity in a precarious industry short on job security for the newly hired.

Since graduating from the training program, demonstrating skills and a work ethic that would make me attractive as a partner to established Merrill Lynch producers was the name of my game. Logistically, the only options for me were the opportunities within the Blueberg branch, so the lay of the land was not hard topography to read. Joining a team was the ticket to job security and, in the right circumstance, a very significant future income. Team membership would deliver me from dependence on the good-heartedness of fellow Blueberg compatriots.

The Blueberg office included several existing teams: Mike Bling and Hank Patton; Sam Reagan and Ted Tiller; Richard Rutledge and Rudy Mantooth; Emily Smith and Tom Hawkins; and Reggie Sparks and Harley Johnson. The obvious choice for me was to pair up with Bill Mitchell, with his massive number of accounts and no partner. The other possibility, which did not interest me, was a partnership with Herb Camp.

There were many good reasons why Herb Camp had been with the firm for seven years and had no prospects of teaming with any other financial advisors. Herb was possibly the laziest person I have ever worked with. Arriving each morning around ten thirty, Herb moseyed through the door just in time to make a couple of personal phone calls and go to lunch with the wholesaler. The paper-thin walls that separated my closet from his office made me privy to the way he conducted his business, no matter how hard I tried to ignore the goings-on of my neighbor.

To make matters worse, Herb, Bill Mitchell, and I had to share Lucy Stone's services. Incensed at having to field Herb's phone calls each day before his arrival, Lucy was often out of sorts before the morning was long under way. I bore the brunt of her moodiness since Bill and his million-dollar production numbers were always handled with care.

Herb's constant neglect of his clients was the bane of Lucy's existence. I could hardly blame her for being frustrated. Although he aggravated me, I did benefit from Herb's business habits. Every client who threatened to leave the firm due to Herb's neglect was promptly transferred to me by Hank. I received three or four very nice accounts this way.

The fact that I was inheriting Herb's dissatisfied clients was the source of some tension between us. Another source of tension was that my relationship with Coach Ford had dethroned Herb as the office's sole purveyor of college football inside information. Herb was envious to the core of my relationship with the coach.

The other fact about Herb, acknowledged by everyone in the office, was his inability to have a short conversation. Herb would keep clients in his office for hours when any other FA would have conducted the meeting in fifteen minutes. It was so bad that FAs in the office wanting to communicate with Herb would often preface the conversation by stating a predetermined time for ending the dialogue.

As an old friend, on more than one occasion Hank had stood between Herb and the Merrill Lynch firing squad. Somehow Herb had managed to hang on for seven years by the skin of his teeth.

As for other potential partners, my experience with Rudy and Richard precluded them from consideration, although I liked them both. They were great guys to hang out with at lunch and banter about nonsense while noontime barbs were being hurled, but these slick industry veterans made me apprehensive. I later learned my instincts were right on target.

As time went by, the circumstances under which Mike Bling and Reggie Sparks had been able to obtain their teammates was revealed to me. Mike Bling actually had to resign and accept a position with Smith Barney to force Hank Patton's hand. Mike worked at Smith Barney for one day. Reggie Sparks had threatened to do the same so management intervened and practically forced Harley Johnson into a partnership with him.

Both Reggie and Mike had hit the jackpot, but the methods they had to employ were disconcerting. I did not want to have to leverage myself into a partnership, particularly with Bill Mitchell, who was somewhat tightfisted anyway. I am sure he would have resented any such move, and starting a partnership on that note would make for some difficult days.

The only other consideration for partnership was Emily Smith. At sixty-five, Tom Hawkins would be sailing into the retirement sunset sometime in the near future. As situations later developed, there would be an opportunity to test-drive a partnership with Emily that would turn out to be a real eye-opener.

My presumed cunning and audacity in bringing in Danny Ford's account, along with some other big successes my first year, made the office sit up and take notice. I could feel a different vibe coming my way, and I liked it. Although I would need help reaching the $15 million goal, I was making as much progress as my peers, if not more. The equilibrium I was finding encouraged me to evaluate my progress in a positive light.

A big part of my newfound confidence grew out of the group lunch experience. There was a strange but good camaraderie that came from having lunch with the office crew three or four times a week. With an office of high-production FAs, the Blueberg outfit was a prime target for mutual fund and annuity wholesalers. An audience with the big producers cost the wholesalers lunch for the entire office, support staff included.

Lunchtime was a political showcase. At eleven thirty every morning Ted Tiller came bolting out of his office for lunch. The place to eat was always a topic of hot debate because some of us liked sushi and some didn't, some liked a certain catering service and some did not. For some unknown reason the job of making the final selection had fallen to Reggie Sparks, and the constant complaints annoyed him to no end. For the really good wholesalers with pertinent information and valuable insight, lunch was held in the conference room, which was light on their expense account while affording the presenter our undivided attention. The conference room was always made available to Mike Gallagher, the wholesaler from PIMCO, as he was far and away the best and most well-informed wholesaler to visit the office regularly.

For the annuity wholesalers, it was a different story. Richard and Rudy often remorselessly hit them for $500 sushi lunches. I grew to love sushi. It was the same old yada, yada, yada with these guys. If we were going to listen to a strictly product-based presentation as opposed to insightful commentary on the markets, it was going to cost them. Such presentations would be made in crowded restaurants, a clever way of limiting the duration.

While the restaurant lunches were not devoid of flair and banter, the conference room affairs were legend. Of all the studying and reading I undertook to learn my craft, nothing prepared me better than these lunches. This is where I learned the lingo of the financial services industry. I had been in attendance at these meetings for six months before I understood exactly what was being said. After I became familiar with the new language, I was able to participate.

The true tale of the tape was the question-and-answer period that followed conference room presentations. Often the discussion turned into heated but friendly debate. Ask a stupid question and you were sure to get slammed. Make an invalid point and correction would come swiftly with the obligatory needling remark attached, especially if Mike Bling was in the room.

It was during these interludes that I discovered my understanding of the issues was more advanced than many others in the room. Sam Reagan, Mike Bling, Reggie Sparks, Richard Rutledge, and Rudy Mantooth were fair and worthy opponents in the field of macroeconomic debate. As far as product knowledge, Bill Mitchell and Harley Johnson were pretty far up the ladder. Ted Tiller, Hank Patton, Herb Camp, and surprisingly Emily Smith were either without opinions or saw no point in leaving themselves open for criticism.

Understanding the lingo was the steepest part of the learning curve, and once this was accomplished, I could validate my discernments about the markets and defend my conclusions with the best of the field. These debates were instrumental in my developing a self-confidence that would play a crucial role during the coming financial crisis.

It was also during these conversations that I absorbed much valuable information about the culture at Merrill Lynch. As Larry McDonald pointed out in his book *A Colossal Failure of Common Sense*, recounting the collapse of Lehman Brothers, big financial corporations rule through fear: "Fear is the key. Fear of being the one person in this whole morass of execs who got it wrong. Fear of being the scapegoat, fear of looking ridiculous, fear of being fired. Thus there develops a whole art form of corporate ducking and diving, staying out of the firing line, writing memorandums somehow shifting the responsibility, not being seen with your head above the parapet, seeking the glory, always dodging the blame, carefully filing the memos that will ultimately exonerate."[2]

Such was the culture at Merrill Lynch and apparently at Smith Barney as well since the veterans of that shop played by the same set of rules. On the other side of that fear coin was greed. The zigzag lines of a stock's price chart are said to illustrate greed and fear.

After deciphering the emotions and motives of my fellow financial advisors, I had to agree with this description of the charts. I had spent my professional life attempting to divorce my decision-making process from these two judgment-impairing emotions. Some voice deep inside warned my psyche of an impending controversy. But the scale of the conflict was obscure and easily pushed to the back of my conscience.

Such was the situation in the summer of 2007. As the insurance continuing education requirement loomed, the moral dilemma it had presented nine months into my Merrill Lynch career two years past had morphed. As the $15 million mountain was just over the horizon, making waves about the moral turpitude of committing fraud over a detail like insurance continuing education would not be in the best interests of my career. The good-old-boy culture demanded I go along to get along. Although I expressed my misgivings and aversion to paying Bruce for services he did not render and lying about having been in class for two days, I acquiesced and participated in the fraud.

I am not proud that I caved in to this pressure, but I did. As a Christian, I am embarrassed that I lacked the faith to stand my ground and let matters take their course. The culture had invaded my morality, and I knew it. I had resolved that in no way would I compromise the fiduciary responsibility I owed my clients,

---

[2] Lawrence G. McDonald, *A Colossal Failure of Common Sense* (New York: Random House, 2009), 57.

but I began to wonder if I would fail that test as well. Instinctively I knew that the test was unavoidably in the offing.

Once I received my production number, the clock was ticking on my quest for the $15 million in assets. Every three months I needed to reach a milestone, and with the help of my fellow financial advisors, I had earned a bonus at each milestone. The first three milestones were fairly reasonable. The milestone at nine months was $10 million. The annual milestone was the end of the rainbow: $15 million in client assets. To gather $5 million in three months was a tall order for even the most experienced financial advisor. For a greenhorn like me, it was to dream the impossible dream.

One month before D-Day, I was forced to approach Hank and break the news that I was not going to achieve the goal. This was not unexpected news. Making that goal in Blueberg would have been headline news within the organization. Hank nevertheless wanted me to achieve graduation from the POA program as soon as possible.

As the twelve-month deadline and the accompanying bonus drew near, the time had run too short for Hank or any other financial advisor to transfer assets into my number for me to qualify for graduation and the $100,000 bonus. At the fifteen-month milestone, we were prepared. This is where Bill Mitchell stepped into the breach on my behalf so I could earn the bonus money and graduate from the POA program.

At fifteen months I would be considered an early graduate of the training program since technically I had twenty-four months to graduate. The downside to graduating was that my salary would disappear and my monthly income would be a draw against future commissions. Failing to cover my draw would bring fire from the business manager, Frank Frazer, in Charlotte. Feeling confident about my abilities and desperately wanting to permanently shed the "pledge" moniker, this was not a hard decision for me.

Although transferring assets from one FA to another was a fairly routine gesture, there was a hitch in the giddy-up. In an accounting sleight-of-hand, Bill Mitchell was going to transfer assets into my number, and once the commissions were paid, I would authorize the transfer of the money back to him. For this to happen, the regional manager, Don Plaus, had to be apprised of the plan. I liked Don. He had been instrumental in helping me land Coach Ford's account. Nevertheless, Don had to maintain that element of fear in all his relationships with FAs. It was the Merrill Lynch way of doing things. As Hank and I made the case for my graduation, Don said, "I am not supposed to know about these things."

In my presence he became quite terse. Hank later told me Don had no real problem with the assets transfer; he just needed plausible deniability in case, down the road, another FA candidate was not given the same consideration for whatever reason.

The meeting we had was in the morning, and shortly after lunch Hank indicated my graduation was in the bag. When Don came to Blueberg, he typically commandeered Hank's office, which was the case this day. As he prepared to leave for Charlotte, I walked back to Hank's office and told Don that in order to deal with him in a straightforward manner, I had to say what I had said.

He shook my hand. I could tell he respected my effort to be transparent, but I also noticed a slight irritation. I got the feeling he expected me to cower in my office until he had left the building.

I had great respect for Don, but I did not fear him. I did not feel I could adequately fulfill my duties to my clients and to the firm while being afraid of management. My attitude was not insubordinate. The opposite was true. I was the team-player type. Years spent in my own company encouraging employees to buy into the organization's future on a personal level had instilled this attitude in me.

At Merrill Lynch I continued to strive to act as part of a team, but in my estimation that did not include fearing management. These two attitudes made me different from all the other financial advisors in the Blueberg office. They weren't buying into anything, and they were petrified of management at the regional director's level. I later would learn why.

My early graduation was a feather in the caps of Paul Pressley, my training coach, Bill Mitchell, my mentor, and Hank Patton, my immediate supervisor. Since the rate of failure is so great, success stories are heralded. I was recognized at the quarterly sales meeting in Charlotte, which made me feel good about my progress in the organization.

But with graduation came the realities of no salary. In retrospect, I knew very little about how financial advisors earned money, and my decision to graduate early was rather careless.

The amount of pay for financial advisors is based off of production credits, or in the vernacular, PCs. Production credits represent income earned by the investment of client assets. Everything revolves around PCs.

To smooth out an FA's cash flow, a draw against commission was available, but failure to cover that draw was the first sign of impending doom. Production credits were the stick by which all advisors were measured. Financial acumen was not rewarded at all. Client investment performance was not rewarded.

Remember that this culture did not care if the financial advisor got it *right*; it was all about getting it *sold*.

When discussing my education concerning the PC learning curve, Reggie Sparks made a comment I'll never forget. He said, "Sometimes this business makes you feel sleazy." I had no idea what he was referring to, but I mulled the comment over and over in my mind until I had to ask Sam, Reggie's best friend, what he had meant by that statement.

All Sam said was, "I can't explain it, but you will understand before long." I could see this was not fodder for the usual office debate or a topic for further discussion. It was clear Sam did not want to talk about it.

To accommodate the strain of no salary, Merrill Lynch paid first-year producers 50 percent of the production credits earned. After one year, this number went to 35 percent but could be increased by generating more PCs. A $1 million producer, for example, could expect to earn up to 50 percent of production. There was also the opportunity to earn a FOG bonus.

FOG is the acronym for Focus on Growth. This was a bonus predicated on new business production. To earn a FOG bonus, the FA had to meet two out of three criteria. One was to bring in two new households for Merrill Lynch with account assets in excess of $250,000. The other two possibilities had to do with net new assets and net new annuitized assets.

The net new annuitized assets are very important to management. Annuitized assets produce income month after month, year after year. Annuitized assets mainly consisted of C-share mutual funds, certain types of annuities, and most importantly, managed money and wrap accounts. Hank Patton was graded in large part by the percentage of financial advisors in the Blueberg office who achieved FOG and how much of the business consisted of recurring sources of income, which was a new focus for the industry.

Another consideration for the experienced advisor is the club level achieved each year. The Circle of Honor and the Chairman's Club are examples of designations achieved by FAs consistently earning more for the firm and deserving recognition. A financial advisor's club level determines the amount of expense money available for entertaining clients, direct mail campaigns, or any other business-related expense. An advisor also receives a nice plaque for the wall, a luxury vacation to the annual meeting, and the esteem of colleagues. Making club is a big deal for all these reasons.

None of this bonus income was tied to investment performance or to any other measure of client service. It does not matter how much money you make for your clients; it only matters how much money you make for the firm.

The industry's move to annuitize client holdings pays the advisor a percentage of the amount of assets under management. The industry would say this provides incentive for advisors to act in their clients' best interests. Since stock positions paid more than bond positions and bond positions paid more than cash, this compensation structure has a built-in conflict of interest. The real fallacy of this assertion did not become evident until the fall of 2008 when advisors faced losing the majority of their income if they chose to protect their clients by moving to cash.

This manner of incentivizing advisors is directly to blame for a culture steeped in conflicts of interest and a disregard for the fiduciary accountability that should be the cornerstone of the industry. As long as one investment earns more for an advisor than another investment, these dynamics will exist within the wealth management industry.

A free market capitalist has ideological problems with paying advisors based on their backslapping ability rather than on an ability to earn higher returns for clients than the competition. Profit is the proper motivation in an economy that creates wealth and a higher standard of living for each succeeding generation. In a true capitalist free market economy, transparency is essential to free and open competition. Only then can capital be allocated properly.

The wealth management side of the financial services industry has developed a culture that hinders the operation of efficient markets. Capital is channeled to the investment paying the highest FA commission, not to the investment offering the best risk/return opportunity. The fundamental misrepresentation made by investment firms to the public concerning their true focus (which is to retain and satisfy financial advisors) ensures a lack of transparency.

In today's marketplace, investors are unaware of the conflicts of interest that invade the relationship with their financial advisor, particularly regarding annuitized assets. The public has only a murky idea of how advisors are paid, and no easy way is accessible for them to find out the truth.

6. Rules of the Road

I'm searchin' for a rainbow,
and if the wind ever shows me where to go,
you'd be waiting at the end, and I know,
I'd see the hill with that pot of gold.

– Toy Caldwell

As a farmer, Coach Ford became interested in biodiesel technology. Through contacts (and Coach Ford has many contacts), he became involved in an effort to build a manufacturing facility for biodiesel fuel in Anderson, South Carolina. After several false starts due to what we now know was a crisis in the financial markets, Coach Ford approached me about funding for the project.

In the course of searching to bring his group a solution, the project mushroomed into a $100 million, multistate funding opportunity for me. To do my job, I had to understand how biodiesel fuel is manufactured and the intricacies of pro forma balance sheets and income statement projections unique to the renewable fuels industry. I learned much about renewable fuels in a short period of time. There were three things about this niche that intrigued me:

- In my professional life I had never worked with farmers, and I found these characters to be a breed apart from any group of business people in my experience.
- I really liked the idea having a hand in helping make our nation energy-independent.
- The income potential from these technologies is astounding.

In my quest to become fluent in the ways and verbiage of the renewable fuels industry, I happened to solicit the aid of Tom Hawkins. One afternoon in late March of 2008, Tom strode into my office with a referral and a possible opportunity for both of us. It seems that his wife had a niece lobbying for the South Carolina renewable fuels industry. She had given Tom's name to Brock Morgan, who was spearheading the fundraising efforts for Ag Renewable Fuels in our state. Ag Renewable Fuels was a corporation seeking $800 million to build ethanol facilities in the states of South Carolina, Georgia, Alabama, and Mississippi.

Brock had called Tom to see if he would recommend the Ag Renewable Fuels investment to some of his clients. Of course, Tom could not make such a recommendation without firm approval. Tom knew I had been putting together funding for the biodiesel project and wondered if I might have any ideas. Not knowing many details, I suggested a meeting with Brock might be in order.

To understand the nature and context in which we were operating, one must recall the events of September 2007. Cracks were beginning to show in our global financial structure during this time, but ambiguity still characterized the economic anomalies that dotted the headlines (the most notable anomaly being an inversion of the U.S. Treasury yield curve).

In the course of my shopping Coach Ford's $100 million biodiesel project, several unexpected obstacles appeared out of nowhere. After meeting with Jeff Kleinfeld of Merrill Lynch Capital from the Charlotte complex, I had been able to generate genuine interest in the biodiesel deal. But shortly after all parties came to an understanding of how we might successfully gain funding, Merrill Lynch Capital was sold to General Electric. This deal made no sense to the grunts in the trenches. "Total Merrill," the branding effort designed to herald the firm's ability to bring our clients a myriad of solutions, was now without a lending source.

Merrill Lynch CEO Stan O'Neal, the architect of the Merrill Lynch debacle, was in the midst of an unsuccessful scramble to save his job. His replacement, John Thain, would spend the fourth quarter of 2007 explaining O'Neal's reckless actions to anxious investors and evaluating the situation within the firm.

The offloading of Merrill Lynch Capital was a sign of things to come. Seeds of doubt were planted within the ranks of the Thundering Herd. The doubt was discussed internally at wholesaler lunches but was considered poisonous for the firm if discussed outside of "the family."

On top of these events, in March of 2008 the Bear Stearns hedge fund fiasco was to bring down that storied investment bank. Industry insiders chalked up the failure to Bear's pot-smoking CEO, Jimmy Cayne. (One day in the elevator at Bear Stearns Cayne had allegedly tried to hand *New York Times* reporter Charlie Gasparino a joint.)[3] Insiders saw the demise of the bank as just desserts for Cayne's failure to participate in the late 1990s rescue of the hedge fund Long-Term Capital Management. At seventy-three, Cayne was the natural scapegoat for the subprime mortgage implosion in March 2008 (which was viewed as contained and certainly not contagious).

Nebulous movements just below the surface on Wall Street occasionally foreshadowed an economic contraction—to what extent was anyone's guess. In early 2006, the U.S. Treasury yield curve had flattened significantly. By the end of 2006 and in early 2007, the yield curve actually inverted. In the financial world, this is the equivalent of seeing the Japanese Navy in early December 1941 trolling the Pacific in the general direction of Pearl Harbor.

The fundamentals of our financial system and the world economy are based on the time value of money. Simply stated, under the ordinary effects of inflation a dollar today is worth more than a dollar a year from today and a lot more than a dollar thirty years from today. But when the interest rate for a three-month loan is greater than the interest rate for a thirty-year loan, debt markets are forecasting a contraction in the economy.

Of course, there was the standard crowd of pundits on the scene to assure us all was well. I remember reading a quote that said that if indeed a recession were to take place, it would be the most predicted recession in history and therefore of minimal impact. The first axiom in the mythical financial advisor handbook is that the stock market is a leading indicator, but the bond market is always right.

Behind the scenes, Wall Street had already begun to implode, but for retail brokers/financial advisors, it was business almost as usual. In retrospect, it is difficult to understand how blinded the industry was to the tectonic shifts moving the platforms we inhabited day in and day out. The signs were there, but they were effectively being explained away by management, analysts, and

---

[3] Charles Gasparino, *The Sellout* (New York: HarperCollins, 2009), 2.

CNBC talking heads. After all, they were smarter than we were, and the "Mad Money" bullishness of CNBC's Jim Cramer kept our clients under control.

But Sam Reagan, Reggie Sparks, and I could not shake the ominous inverted yield curve or the warnings being heralded by David Rosenberg at Merrill Lynch Research. The voices of Bill Gross and Mohammad El-Erian at PIMCO were screeching as well, and those guys actually were the smartest in the room.

It was against this backdrop that on a beautiful April morning in 2008 Tom Hawkins and I headed out to meet with Brock Morgan.

To an outdoorsman like Tom Hawkins, April in South Carolina means turkey season, and Tom Hawkins could call turkeys like they were the family Labrador. Few things distracted Tom from the pursuit of turkeys in April, but the prospect of establishing a lucrative relationship with Ag Renewable Fuels had put the gobblers on his back burner.

Brock had given us directions to his home in quaint little Lukenbach, a place some sixty miles from our Blueberg office. Brock's family had been farming this area since the War Between the States, and as we neared the driveway, we could not help being struck with the beauty of the rolling hills that glistened with the morning's spring dew.

We pulled into the driveway in front of what appeared to be the Morgan family's old homestead. Following the dirt road that wound behind the old house, we entered an even more picturesque setting. A newly constructed house sat tucked on the banks of a large pond. As we made our way to the house, the majesty of the day and the beauty of our surroundings only contributed to the comfort level Tom and I were beginning to develop.

The first time I saw Brock Morgan, he was standing in the gravel driveway of his pond house waiting to greet Tom and me. A tall, handsome man of about fifty-five, Brock had neatly trimmed gray hair and a warm southern smile. He welcomed us, and I immediately noticed his comfortable, confident manner that was to be a constant characteristic of my dealings with him. In the course of our relationship, I witnessed Brock being dealt all kinds of cards, but I never saw him veer from his easygoing, sincere nature.

Once inside the house, Brock introduced us to Frank Cook of Fagan Construction Company. After some small talk, Frank directed our attention to the laptop computer sitting on a pine kitchen table and began the presentation to help Tom and I understand more about Ag Renewable Fuels and their organizational objectives. Fagan Construction had built 75 percent of the corn ethanol facilities now operating in the United States. Frank made a convincing argument for the project now being considered and was obviously capable of answering far more complex questions than either Tom or I could ask.

Ag Renewable Fuels had been formed by four groups seeking independently to bring ethanol production to the states of South Carolina, Georgia, Alabama, and Mississippi. Dr. Edgar Snipes had encouraged and then facilitated combining their efforts into Ag Renewable Fuels. Snipes, who was involved with a group that owned an ethanol plant currently under construction by Fagan, was a college professor/researcher/politico/farmer in Lower Alabama. Since Dr. Snipes was the chairman of the board of Ag Renewable Fuels, the natural extension of his relationship with Fagan had brought Frank Cook to Brock Morgan's pond house this April morning to promote this new, much more ambitious undertaking.

Not being fully conversant with the jargon of the renewable fuels industry with respect to ethanol left me a little foggy on some of the project details being explained. As Tom and I were briefed, Tom suddenly stood up and started pacing back and forth. He explained that he had difficulty sitting still for any long period of time. There was an awkward pause before we moved ahead with the presentation.

From what I could understand, Ag Renewable Fuels had discovered a logistical advantage in shipping corn to the ethanol production facilities they wanted to build as opposed to shipping ethanol to southeastern distribution points. The logistical advantage had to do with the byproduct of ethanol production, dried distillers grain (DDG), which is a mineral-rich feed for farm animals. Having this byproduct easily accessible to poultry farmers and livestock ranchers created a significant efficiency in the supply chain.

Both Brock and Frank demonstrated that the efficiency was quite significant, or at least they made the attempt. Before I could get comfortable in my chair, the discussion was over my head, and after thirty minutes of the presentation, I was just trying to hang on.

I did grasp the main points of the business plan, but certain things made me sit up and take notice, things that had nothing to do with the nuts and bolts of making ethanol in Mississippi. These guys knew what they were talking about, even if they could not explain it to Tom and me. They obviously believed fervently in the plan, and the numbers they were using had been provided by a Midwest accounting firm that handled the books for most of the ethanol industry (government numbers have always left me suspicious). They also had legal representation from Iowa, who I suspected knew a thing or two about corn.

The other thing I was discerning had to do with the nuts and bolts. Fagan Construction Company was willing to guarantee one gallon of ethanol per 2.6 bushels of corn introduced into the manufacturing process. Even Tom and I could understand how important this was, and Fagan was willing to back it up with a guarantee in writing.

Becoming educated enough to make a determination as to the legitimacy of this proposal was going to require a large investment of my time and was, frankly, beyond my purview at Merrill Lynch. I had only recently shed my pledge badge, and the typical path to success for advisors in my position was not working on projects like this. But then again, the typical path to success for advisors in my position had disappeared with the do-not-call list.

As we drove back to Blueberg, it occurred to me how much more comfortable I was than Tom in the setting we had just left. Thirty-two years of dispensing advice on stocks to physicians and selling annuities to the recently retired had not prepared him for the experience. By contrast, my experience making presentations to CEO-level management in the selling of commercial insurance coverage had provided me with experience in many similar situations in the past.

As I mentally evaluated the big picture, I intuitively started drawing the conclusion that the Ag Renewable Fuels guys were both smart and genuine. In my mind those are the two indispensable ingredients in any mutually beneficial business relationship. In light of the industry change brought about by the do-not-call list issues, this deal offered an opportunity to hit a home run in a ballpark I had played in before.

Even though the tenor of the discussion had been vague, I knew I wanted to move forward, and as I looked into the eyes of Tom Hawkins, I could see he was unsuccessfully suppressing his own excitement. After all, we had just been asked to evaluate an $800 million, multistate deal involving some of the biggest players in the U.S. renewable energy space. The tentacles of this opportunity stretched over four states and into some deep pockets, never mind the fact that it would be the largest deal originating in South Carolina that Merrill Lynch had ever facilitated. Tom and I rightfully had something to be excited about.

The very fact that Tom Hawkins and Hal Blackwell from Blueberg, South Carolina, were being asked to evaluate this deal should have been a foghorn alert that the capital markets were in shambles. There was, however, an apparently logical explanation for our good fortune: Midwest farmers had stood in line to buy shares in new ethanol production enterprises just months ago. That had all changed due to the developing financial crisis. Maybe Tom and I were just fortunate to be riding the crest of this wave of change. After all, Merrill Lynch was still touting our ability to offer a "Total Merrill" solution to prospective clients' needs. We had no reason to doubt the veracity of these insistent claims coming from management.

The government had mandated the blending of ethanol into the nation's fuel supply, and it was also an adequate substitute for an environmentally unacceptable additive that had been banned nationwide. With gasoline at $4 a gallon and a barrel of oil selling for $140, ethanol was cheaper than fossil fuels. Finding investors for ethanol projects in this pre-crisis environment had been a simple matter of advertising the opportunity.

Ag Renewable Fuels had planned the same capital-raising activities the ethanol producers had deployed in the Midwest. In the summer of 2008, market dynamics had changed; a barrel of oil was $100 and heading down to $32, but the price of corn was still elevated, which made for some tough sledding in the ethanol business. Ag Renewable Fuels could not have picked a more difficult environment in which to launch such a campaign. Because of these new dynamics, a happenstance phone call to Tom Hawkins had given us a shot at the big leagues. Now it was time for us to show some smarts and the determination to capitalize on our good fortune.

In order to get a better handle on the financial side, as opposed to the technical side that Brock and Frank Cook had so artfully presented, we were referred to Derek Cannon of D. Cannon and Associates, an advisory firm (Derek detests the term consultant although that is what he is) located in Atlanta. Derek had been hired by Ag Renewable Fuels to secure funding for the project.

Tom, Emily Smith, and I arranged to meet him halfway between Blueberg and Atlanta. At the meeting, we found him to be professional, prepared, and thoroughly versed in the current conditions within the capital markets. He was anxious to hear what we had to offer, which, frankly, was not much.

I took the lead in explaining to Derek how we would present the project to Merrill Lynch Global Private Equity (MLGPE) in New York. Not being an investment banker, and having only my biodiesel fuel experience to rely upon, my message was simply a description of the process within Merrill Lynch we would try to deploy on ARF's behalf. The amount of information we had to offer Derek left much to be desired, and I'm sure he wondered if his trip from Atlanta had been a waste of time.

After the meeting and subsequent phone calls, I was able to arrange for Emily and I to make a presentation at the next ARF board meeting. Emily and Tom were not expecting a rookie FA to be so bold as to ask for time at a meeting of the board of directors. All Emily could say was, "Way to go, Hal," and she said it several times. Asking to address the board seemed like the logical next step to me, but Emily's reaction indicated a different philosophy in approaching prospective clients.

The next board meeting was to be held early in May in Jasper Hills, Alabama, about two hundred and fifty miles from Blueberg. On the appointed morning, Emily and I set out together on the long drive.

Emily is an extremely intelligent person with whom I had earned favor early on in our relationship. Shortly after she and Tom had made their great escape from Smith Barney, I, being a relatively unknown newcomer, had volunteered to retrieve Emily's belongings from her former office. The employees at Smith Barney were expecting me and pointed to a box of personal file folders and a stack of pictures that had obviously been on Emily's office wall. Retreating back across enemy lines to the safety of Merrill Lynch, I presented Emily with her precious belongings, which brought her obvious gratification and relief.

Gleefully she hung the framed pictures and documents on her new office wall. Prominently displayed was her Phi Beta Kappa award, hung beside her magna cum laude degree, which hung beside her postgraduate degree, which hung beside various other certificates of academic achievement. There was no doubt about it, Emily had credentials.

She also frequently wore an intentionally low neckline and leggy skirts that bordered on inappropriate. She had strategically enhanced her granola look by accentuating an extremely lean and athletic figure. Emily was too smart to accidentally be provocative, and it wasn't hard to see that she carried all her weapons to the battlefield.

The day we set out for Jasper Hills, Emily was loaded for bear.

It's always a little unnerving when you make a four-hour drive and are ten minutes late. Such was the case this day as Emily and I struggled to find the remote location for the board of directors' lunch meeting where we were to make our pitch for the Ag Renewable Fuels account. Since most farmers live in the boondocks and like to hold meetings in the boondocks, working with them can be a geographic challenge. There aren't boonier boondocks than those in Lower Alabama.

Although I was unaware at the time, I soon learned that farmers must have a diversified skill set. Knowing how to grow stuff, keeping animals thriving, hedging commodity markets, and measuring political bets, along with having various and sundry personal skills, all go together to make the complete farmer.

These fifteen guys also knew talent when they saw it. Emily's cleavage and short skirt helped them overlook the fact that we were ten minutes late. That day I received a firsthand demonstration of the initial phase of Emily's account acquisition strategy. Her presentation on the mechanics of Merrill Lynch's business money-management account was articulate and well informed, but to the board members her countenance made her memorable and effective. I was learning.

When it was my turn to woo the crowd, I turned to a tactic sure to please in Lower Alabama. Instead of conjuring up some exaggeration of my experience or making promises I probably couldn't keep, I simply opted for telling the truth. Fortunately for me in those parts, that truth included a story, told with permission, about my relationship with Coach Danny Ford. Regardless of the fact that these men had gathered from four different states, it would have been difficult to come up with another person with more appeal to this group than Coach Ford.

Within the limitations of client confidentiality, and with complete confidence, I explained the depth of my experience with biodiesel projects. It did not take long. My grandfather used to say, "It doesn't take long to tell the truth, and you don't have to remember what you said." Since I had a bad memory and no cleavage, my options were few.

After the meeting we returned to the office. Through a couple of phone calls in search of feedback on our presentation, I learned that our competitors were Morgan Stanley and an unidentified bank. Over the next month, I had extensive conversations with Derek Cannon and Brock Morgan. As negotiations dragged on, Emily and Tom went back to their daily routines of constructing portfolios, doing client reviews, completing annuity applications, and selling stocks.

In the meantime, Derek and I had built a rapport, and I was considering introducing him to Coach Ford and some of the other big players in the biodiesel space (one of Willie Nelson's partners had become a client of mine). These contacts had real potential to offer synergies for all concerned, but until we had a verdict on the Ag Renewable Fuels deal, I only hinted to Derek of the possibilities.

Falling back into a routine was not an option for me. In late 2007 and early 2008, Merrill Lynch and its Thundering Herd of financial advisors came under siege. The Merrill Lynch news was frequent, bad, and on the front page. It all started in October 2007 when CEO Stan O'Neal resigned after the firm lost billions of dollars in the third quarter. O'Neal's transgressions were many: purchasing First Franklin at the top of the mortgage-market bubble, his practice of

warehousing mortgages, leveraging the balance sheet forty to one, and alienat-
ing most of the firm's top talent in the middle of a credit crisis, just to name a
few.

To make matters worse, before his departure O'Neal had the audacity to
shop the firm to Wachovia behind the back of the Merrill Lynch board of directors. The magnitude of O'Neal's folly was to unfold over the course of late
2007 and all of 2008, but the immediate manifestation of his leadership fiasco
came in the form of third-quarter earnings reports that included write-downs
denominated in billions of dollars (that was back in the old days, when losing a
billion carried a stigma).

After reporting record revenue in the second quarter, these startling third-
quarter results put Merrill Lynch in the spotlight and kicked off a pundits' play-
by-play commentary of the downward spiral engulfing the firm's stock price.
A more brutal environment for soliciting the trust of potential clients was not
possible—or at least so I thought until later events turned these headlines into
footnotes.

Nevertheless, I had a plan. Although the Ag Renewable Fuels account was
not going to be full of C-share mutual funds (great commission generators), an
$800 million inflow of cash would be big enough to make a difference. Holding
that kind of money just for the time between ARF's deposit of the funds and the
disbursements to cover construction costs would earn the firm $700,000, of
which the financial advisors would get roughly 40 percent. The initial deal was
worth $140,000 to me, after the split with Emily and Tom.

The average balance of $50 million in the Ag Renewable Fuels working capi-
tal account would provide us each approximately $25,000 per year in income
and would surely help earn bonus money. After the trades ARF would regularly
execute to hedge corn and ethanol pricing, the account would be considered
significant by anyone's standards.

Shortly after lunch on a hot June day, my phone rang with a call from Brock
Morgan. He had good news. Based on what the board of directors had perceived
as a straightforward and transparent presentation in Jasper Hills coupled with
the vast amount of follow-up work I had done, Ag Renewable Fuels had decided
to open an account and deposit several million dollars with Merrill Lynch. They
asked if I would proceed with the applications to Merrill Lynch Global Private
Equity and Merrill Lynch Venture Capital to seek the $800 million funding
required by the project.

Since the presentation in Jasper Hills, my discussions with Brock Morgan and
Derek Cannon had included a detailed outline of the funding markets available

at our company. The prerequisite for consideration by the funding sources was the establishment of an account in the Blueberg office of Merrill Lynch.

With the news of our Ag Renewable Fuels success, I realized I now had two new partners. But there was one issue that needed addressing sooner rather than later. My agreement with Emily and Tom was for a 50/25/25 split on the deal, and all parties had that understanding. But as Derek and I discussed Ag Renewable Fuels, other opportunities had become evident.

I saw no reason to discuss these matters with Tom and Emily.

Money has a way of attracting money, but it also has a way of attracting vultures. It was imperative that the terms of my relationship with Tom and Emily take a written form. Having a source of expertise like Derek could bring in significant assets for Merrill Lynch and the financial advisor smart enough to properly leverage the relationship.

I was not sure how these opportunities would develop, but I was learning from watching Derek negotiate multimillion-dollar deals that one thing was for certain: my arrangement with the Smith/Hawkins team had to be squared away. I figured that if I hung around the barbershop with Derek long enough, I would wind up with a mighty nice haircut. Now I had to make sure Emily Smith didn't make off with my scalp first.

My arrangement with Emily and Tom was definitely a fly in the ointment, with Emily more than with Tom. In the financial services industry, an introduction entitled an FA to part of the deal. As a team, Tom and Emily were entitled to half of the Ag Renewable Fuels account even though they had not interacted with anyone working on the deal for two months. Strategically, I thought determining the split on future deals would be best negotiated during a period of Emily and Tom's gratitude to me for presenting them with the gift embodied by the Ag Renewable Fuels success.

Since Tom was out of the office, I delivered the good news to Emily. She was caught by surprise but thrilled at the prospect of working on this account. Not only did the opportunity represent the Ag Renewable Fuels account, but it also represented access to all of the high net worth seed investors and an opportunity to solicit their business. Having access to one hundred and twenty juicy accounts was potentially a career-changer. The upside of this transaction was enormous, and I had just handed it to Emily on a silver platter, as I had agreed to do.

After discussing some of the logistics, I mentioned to Emily that we needed to solidify the commission splits on the various tentacles represented by our new account. At a meeting in Tom's office later that day, it became evident that

Emily's gratitude had a short shelf life. She became focused on claiming 50 percent of any other deals emanating from this transaction and/or my relationship with Derek.

In effect, she wanted me to work for her. She had no illusions regarding her difficulty bringing value to clients in this arena, no concept of what was required to move the process forward, and no context for understanding the roles of the different players or what motivated each one. She was under the impression that because my introduction to Derek had come through Tom, industry protocol entitled her and Tom to half of everything.

I was taken aback at this blatant display of greed and never considered moving forward under the arrangement she insisted was standard and fair in the wealth management world. Calmly but assertively, I suggested what I considered to be a fair split, but since it did not include paying her for deals I carried to Derek, she was outraged at my perceived attempt to cut her out.

A meeting that had started with much camaraderie ended on a tense exchange. Flabbergasted by such voracity and shortsightedness and wanting to thrash out the issues and come to an understanding, I agreed to a meeting two days later in Hank Patton's office.

I knew Emily would insist on a 50 percent cut of every deal that ran through Derek. While Tom and Emily were rightfully due 50 percent of any deals coming from Derek, they had no right, in my view, for any part of any deals that I took to Derek. The first rule of negotiating is to never lose your walking-away power, and I reminded myself of this before the looming meeting.

On entering Hank's office, I noticed immediately that Emily had positioned herself in front of Hank's desk and that Tom had taken a position to the left of Hank such that he was almost sitting behind Hank's desk with him. The only empty chair was to Emily's right, at the corner of Hank's desk, facing Hank and Tom.

Positioning in any negotiation is always important, but from the looks of things, the duo had taken no time to consider the seating arrangement. The moment I sat down in the chair, I had Tom and Emily separated.

Even though Hank was sitting behind his desk, the way Tom was situated mitigated the power usually associated with the position. Unwittingly, they had left me the power seat in room, and I came prepared to use it.

Once I sat down, everyone exchanged brief pleasantries, and we then moved on to the business at hand. I stated my view, and then Emily grabbed the floor and began her prosecution. True to her academic persuasion, Emily pulled from her stack of notes a list of yes-or-no questions I am sure she painstakingly designed to drive home her point. She planned to paint me into a corner and then claim the prize that, in her mind, she so richly deserved.

I knew if Emily were not acquainted with every detail pertaining to the deal when she scheduled this meeting, the two subsequent days had provided ample time for a meticulous review by such an accomplished academic. I suspected the stack of paper in her lap was the yield from her research.

I remembered a conversation we once had where she said, "Hal, you may know more about history and economics than I do, but if it ever came down to a strategy game, I'd kick your ass." There was no question in my mind that Emily had something to prove, and this stage was her perfect proving ground.

With the exception of Don Plaus and his compliance director Don Minor, everyone I interacted with at Merrill Lynch was afflicted with an incredible inability to see beyond a certain focal point in any given situation. It had nothing to do with intelligence, but I think it had everything to do with experience. The financial services industry had indoctrinated these people with a paradigm that severely limited their ability to think beyond certain parameters. As we sat there having this give-and-take, it occurred to me that none of the people in the room with me understood that I held all the cards in this game.

After our meeting in Jasper Hills, I had come together with Tom and Emily to flesh out a course of action that they disagreed with. In their minds, business was obtained by first doing things to get the prospect to like you personally, and then imposing on them as a financial advisor to do a favor by letting Merrill Lynch handle their account. Conversely, I operated by learning as much about the prospect as possible to understand their needs, both perceived and unperceived. Once the prospect's needs were defined and identified, my method was to establish a very clear understanding with the prospect that if I demonstrated an ability to meet those needs, I expected to be hired. Once I had this agreement, I could start being creative in finding intelligent, well-conceived solutions that made my relationship very valuable to the prospect.

Financial advisors tend to consider their services ubiquitous, and they are right if prospective clients see them as replaceable. I always thought that if you consider yourself easily replaced, the client sooner or later subliminally gets the message and agrees with you.

I considered my clients lucky to have me as their advisor because I worked my tail off to be better than the rest. I figured it was just a matter of time until word got around. I know that may sound arrogant, but I planned to build my business by offering real value to my clients. I was simply trying to outwork the competition.

Emily and Tom agreed with my strategy of identifying a prospect's needs but felt asking for a commitment and then holding the prospect accountable was crass. They considered my methods terribly aggressive, and their look as I explained how to execute such a plan made it clear that they thought it had no chance of success.

Due to my previous experience, Ag Renewable Fuels had chosen to deal with me as their go-to person, so I decided to forego the laborious debate with Tom and Emily on strategy and instead decided to move forward on my own in my dealings with the company.

In this meeting with Hank, Emily protested that she had not been asked to do anything or provide any input on the account, which was true. I countered that, in the end, my methods had proven effective and that battling Tom and her at every turn on every decision would have been counterproductive.

After ten minutes of this give-and-take, it was obvious Emily and Tom had prepped Hank and that he was there to witness Emily's prosecution and at the appropriate moment render judgment in their favor. Emily and Tom were much bigger earners than I was. They also had a special place in Hank's heart because of their defection from Smith Barney. I accepted this reality and took no offense, but in the end, I still held all the cards.

When Emily, in her best prosecutorial inflection, asked her first question, I immediately objected to the tone and told the group I was not going participate in Emily's premeditated interrogation. I expressed to Hank my dismay at Emily's lack of gratitude and briefly described to Hank how she and Tom had made practically no contribution to the consummation of the deal. I pointed out that they had no idea what had transpired or any concept of the amount of work I had invested in the project.

Since Emily continually attempted to return to her list of questions, I was forced to play my cards in an effort to add some perspective for Hank. I told the group that I would respectfully bow out. I insisted that 50 percent of the ARF account was mine but that I would make arrangements with Brock and Derek to be excluded going forward. I told them I had many other irons in the fire and that they were welcome to begin their "relationship approach" to take the account where they saw fit. I wished them good luck.

At this juncture, the tables were turned, and everyone in the room knew it. Tom immediately suggested a cooling off period and expressed a determination to reach an accommodation acceptable to all. Hank was observing and seemed to be gauging whether or not I was bluffing. I wasn't. Emily, seeing her best laid plans disintegrate, adopted a completely new demeanor and tone of voice, and the fervor to ask her crafty questions evaporated. The whole episode left me mildly upset but educated regarding several aspects of this industry on several levels.

I think Hank had harbored ambitions of possibly teaming me with Tom and Emily for the long term. Because I was from Folksy and their book of accounts consisted of many people I had known since childhood, this might have been fitting a round peg into a round hole. I made it clear in the meeting, however, that such a partnership would no longer be possible. That was probably a tactical error, but the conflict between us made it true. Like it or not, Emily and I were going to be working on the ARF account together, and my straightforwardness about not wanting to team with her only added to the bad feelings. This was not in the best interests of the client, so that made it a mistake on my part.

From a twenty-thousand-foot perspective, viewing the big picture of the wealth management industry, this set of events added significant context to my understanding of what I was up against at Merrill Lynch. Clearly FAs were not bashful about accepting credit or money for services not provided. Such overt greed was shocking and beyond anything in my experience.

In my view, Emily's greed made her untrustworthy. Extrapolating the fact that Hank was not affected by Emily's display, one could reasonably assume her attitude was indigenous to the culture, which shocked me even more. For the first time, I became fully cognizant of the unscrupulous limits of FA behavior and resolved to constantly remind myself of the nature of my competition.

In the following days, Emily, Tom, and I came to an agreement. I would share 50/50 with Emily and Tom on accounts emanating from the seed investors with Ag Renewable Fuels. Any new deals coming from Derek would pay 80/20 in my favor. On deals I initiated with Derek, Emily and Tom would have no claim to payment and no say in how the account was handled. Most importantly, it was established that I would dictate policy and be consulted in any contact with Ag Renewable Fuels.

As we moved forward in servicing the account, Emily showed the core competence that had decorated her wall with accolades. She was precise and consistent in setting up the necessary accounts for Ag Renewable Fuels. While not overly endowed with an ability to figure out how various players in a deal are motivated, Emily is gifted in her ability to come up with actions to accomplish a particular goal. Interacting with the administrative person at Ag Renewable Fuels, she had no equal, and with her new attitude of respect and cooperation, my job was to erase any hard feelings that had developed.

My initial assessment of Emily's greed was to some extent mitigated as we worked together. What I had construed as greed was probably a combination of greed and, to a large extent, a well-disguised insecurity. The paper on Emily's wall made for an enduring and well-constructed camouflage that masked a level of self-doubt she would never admit to having. Understanding this about Emily allowed me to work with her on a daily basis, but I always kept my eyes peeled for anything that looked suspicious.

7. Getting Lucky

You gotta pay your dues
If you want to sing the blues
And you know it don't come easy.

– Richard Starkey

With the opening of the business account, Merrill Lynch would now make available to Ag Renewable Fuels the other resources of the firm. ARF thus qualified to have me send the necessary documents to Merrill Lynch Global Private Equity in New York, as I'd promised would be our first order of business. Emily helped me fill out the online questionnaire, and full of hope we submitted it on June 1, 2008. The response from MLGPE in New York should have clued us in to the shrouded turmoil that had by now gripped our firm.

Despite compelling data arranged professionally, after a few days MLGPE sent back the decline notice we had on some level expected. We fared no better with the venture capital liaison for Merrill Lynch located in Farmington Hills, Michigan. On both counts the explanation was a lack of interest in the ethanol space.

At the time of our submission, the price of corn and of ethanol had significantly changed the economics of the project from what we had originally envisioned. The spread that had enticed Midwestern corn farmers to line up for miles to invest in ethanol production facilities was gone. Additionally, many of the plants already constructed were experiencing difficulties due to heavy debt loads and glitches associated with starting up the manufacturing process. This left a significant portion of domestic production capability underutilized.

Even though the situation had changed and ethanol investments had lost their shine, MLGPE too quickly brushed aside our proposal. Had the project been given due consideration, more questions would have been forthcoming from one of these shops in New York or Michigan. It is hard to put a finger on what aroused my suspicions, but the way in which it was handled and the perfunctory wording of the communication, not expected for a project this size, made me uneasy. I was sure something wasn't right.

Not long after I delivered the bad news to Ag Renewable Fuels, I received a phone call that was to shape the rest of my career at Merrill Lynch. From Hartsville International Airport in Atlanta, Derek Cannon called me with a simple question: Did I know anyone in Dubai? Derek explained that he and Dr. Snipes were boarding a plane headed for Dubai. They were implementing the Willie Sutton strategy for locating money. Derek wanted to know if I knew anybody where the money was. Knowing that Merrill Lynch had an office in Dubai, I instinctively said yes, and I promised to make a call on their behalf.

Due to the time of day in Dubai, the phone call could not be made immediately. I looked up our office there and found the name of Anthony Rawlinson. Via e-mail, I gave Anthony a brief description of the situation and asked him to call me at a designated time. Right on the minute, the phone rang, and I introduced myself to the Dubai Merrill Lynch office. Of Middle Eastern descent, Anthony spoke with a British accent and was mannerly but to the point.

After I explained in more detail who Derek and Dr. Snipes were and that they would soon be contacting him, Anthony realized Derek had just called. I fervently vouched for my clients and assured Anthony that they were exactly who they claimed to be. During the course of the conversation, it became evident that Anthony had blown off Dr. Snipes and Derek as just another inquiry from probing Americans. On understanding the real situation, he excitedly volunteered to call them to arrange a meeting.

After I hung up the phone, it occurred to me that Anthony had no idea who I was or what my responsibilities at Merrill Lynch might be. Admittedly, I did nothing to discourage any notion he might have that I was a big player on this side of the pond in the renewable energy industry at Merrill Lynch. It also occurred to me that once Dr. Snipes and Derek were accommodated by Anthony, they might develop a similar notion. It also occurred to me that at that moment I had stepped through a passage and was now playing on an international field and interacting with some of its biggest players. The prospects of where this might take me were pretty doggone exciting, and I had to chuckle at just how plain lucky I had been to get this far down the road.

After their meeting, Anthony called to give me an update. He had a connection that might put ARF on the fast track to getting their project funded.

But there was one more dragon to slay. Fontaine Capital, an investment bank headquartered in London, was interested in the deal, but Merrill Lynch did not have an agreement in place by which any of us might get paid on such a transaction. Anthony had no qualms with the arrangement because he wanted to enhance his relationship with Fontaine Capital. His concern was my throwing a monkey wrench in the gears by demanding payment.

My reply was instantaneous. There was nothing to think about. By no means would I do anything to hamper ARF's efforts. As I unhesitatingly made the pronouncement, the recollection of Emily's performance in Hank's office came to mind. This was no time for greedy, shortsighted discussions or decisions, and the thought of getting Emily's input passed into my mind and out again immediately. We had all agreed to be paid for managing the money once it arrived at Merrill Lynch, and there would be no straying off course now. I was so thankful I had control of this decision.

I delivered the news, and to my surprise, neither Emily nor Tom was upset. Emily's reaction was to encourage me, and I felt like it was genuine. She may not have realized that the standard fee on a deal that size would have been in the neighborhood of $7 million, but it didn't matter because the discussion never took place.

Once home, Derek and the board of ARF decided to engage Fontaine Capital in arranging international funding. Onto the playing field stepped Mosh Singho, Fontaine's man in Dubai. Educated at Oxford and the veteran of many venture capital deals, Mosh understood that Indian, Chinese, and Middle Eastern businesspeople were looking for opportunities to own American businesses. This was particularly the case if a significant portion of the investment included U.S. real estate.

Mosh immediately went to work arranging the funding of ARF for the astronomically large sum of $800 million. What portion of this would be equity and what portion would be debt was to be negotiated as potential investors were vetted and a deal cobbled together.

ARF was attempting to raise $800 million in the worst capital markets since the Great Depression. In February 2008, prior to the Bear Stearns fire sale to J.P. Morgan, a mysterious yet dramatic development occurred behind the curtain of the financial industry.

Auction rate securities (ARS) are investments that were considered, for all intents and purposes, to be as liquid as cash. Actually, they were securitized debt backed up by many different AAA-rated debt instruments, revalued so frequently in the market that they were considered "cash" on corporate and institutional balance sheets.

These little-known instruments were traded between banks, corporations, and high net worth individuals, some resetting interest rates every seven days and others on a thirty-day cycle. Prior to February 2008, it was inconceivable that the auction for these securities might fail. But that is exactly what happened, setting off an ominous chain of events behind the scenes on Wall Street that eventually spilled onto Main Street.

Financial advisors at Merrill Lynch were told that ARS investments were the safest anywhere. Occasionally, as a favor to large clients (there was little or no commission on an ARS trade), I would glance at the market and purchase a limited amount of these securities for my most valued clients.

Incredibly, when these markets froze, Merrill Lynch management was able to explain away the phenomena as an anomaly and nothing more. While other FAs were angry about being misled and having to call their best clients in an attempt to allay any fears, Emily and I were about to encounter a unique set of problems one can only surmise was due to the financial system's evaporation of liquidity.

Near the end of July, to build troop morale, Don Plaus paid a visit to Blueberg. Don had replaced Scott Hotham as regional director and was now Hank Patton's immediate supervisor. Having worked for Don in the past, Hank was quick to describe him as old-school. "Plaus is all about the numbers," he would say.

Despite a one-year defection to Morgan Stanley, Don was held in the highest esteem by the Blueberg troops. All the women in the office swooned over the handsome figure he cut, a piece of information I could have gone without knowing, but it was an emotional scar I carried from life in the cube. In contrast to Scott Hotham, who only visited the office rarely, Don came by almost monthly under normal circumstances, but now he was making more frequent appearances.

At the announcement of his pending arrival, which was usually made via e-mail two days in advance, the office took on a different vibe. It was an atmosphere of apprehension with maybe a smidgen of respect as everyone puckered up to kiss the royal you-know-what. I just made sure my desk was neat, but cluttered enough to look like a hub of activity.

On this visit I brought Don up to date with respect to the relationship between Fontaine Capital and ARF. I told him there would be a conference call later that morning with my contacts at ARF and asked if he could participate. I knew that Don, along with other members of management, considered this project to be pie-in-the-sky. After all, how could an FA with such limited experience be involved in a legitimate project of this size?

After the call, Don was a believer. His immediate concern was the legitimacy of Fontaine Capital. He straightaway called New York, reaching across the organizational chart to corroborate the correctness and wisdom of Anthony Rawlinson's decision to engage Fontaine. When the message came back from London confirming Fontaine Capital's position as a legitimate investment bank (one Merrill Lynch was seeking to do business with), Don's attitude changed abruptly in our favor.

As Don began using his authority to marshal the forces of Merrill Lynch on behalf of our client, I could not help but smile at my newfound credibility. He noticed and made a remark I will never forget. Leaning back in Hank's office chair, he said caustically, "What are you smiling about?"

"I've never done a $400 million deal before."

"It hasn't happened yet," he replied.

After he realized the tone of his comments, he tried for the remainder of the day to mitigate what he had said. In no way did I let on that the comment affected me. My philosophy has always been that you never, ever let 'em see you sweat (if you can avoid it). I think this is what peeved Don though he would never admit it.

While consciously being completely respectful, I always spoke my mind when asked a question. As a man of faith, I was relying on a power greater than Don Plaus. Our conversations were different than the brownnosing back and forth he was receiving from the other FAs. Our relationship made Hank Patton nervous, and it obviously perturbed Don to a degree. He liked to be brownnosed.

I had bought into the company line that Merrill Lynch was a meritocracy. After all, that is what my screen saver heralded every morning from my desktop computer. I figured that as long as my efforts showed potential to earn income for the firm, or actually earned income for the firm, and as long as I played by the rules and demonstrated a passionate desire to treat my clients as I would want to be treated, my employment status at Merrill Lynch would be secure.

I was wrong on this score and would later pay a price for my naïveté. Nevertheless, there was no question that I had earned Don's respect. The acquisition of Coach Ford's account and the ARF deal lent me a credibility no one could deny, and even Don Plaus had to admit that, my clean nose notwithstanding, I was making notable progress for a recent trainee.

On this morning of his enlightenment, Don did assume a certain ownership of the ARF project. My impression was that he was trying to play catch-up so that if the deal went big, his fingerprints would be all over it. When Merrill Lynch London said Fontaine Capital passed muster, they also relayed that the firm was not going to be paid. Don's first focus was on gauging the wiggle room on the pay issue. He was going to see if the firm (along with he, Emily, Tom, and I) could be paid on the Fontaine Capital transaction.

After making some inquiries, he called me back to Hank's office to ask what arrangements I had made on getting everyone paid. His intonation inferred that I had made a stupid decision, being involved in a deal out of my league. I got the sense he wanted me to renege on the arrangement I had agreed to with Mosh and Anthony. But my word is my bond. I had made an agreement, and I wasn't going to go back on it even if Merrill Lynch decided to fire me.

Don could tell by the confidence in my voice that there was no ambiguity he might leverage in the arrangements I had made with Fontaine Capital. It seemed he was dying to say that an FA in Blueberg did not have the authority to waive a $7 million fee on behalf of Merrill Lynch.

Before that ball started rolling down the hill, I pointed out that Anthony and I had unhesitatingly acted in the best interests of our client. Had we insisted on being paid the transaction fee the project would not have been considered until Merrill Lynch and Fontaine Capital ironed out an agreement. My position was that the client should not be penalized because we had no agreement in place and no other option. I have to admit Anthony Rawlinson's support was very comforting. He did have the authority to waive the fee and I was simply agreeing with a course of action Anthony had laid out. His experience and judgment was unassailable even by Don Plaus.

I explained the dilemma Anthony had presented to me and how I arrived at the decision to forgo payment on the transaction. He then asked how we were going to make money on the deal.

I pointed out that fifty basis points on $400 million equals $2 million. I also said that the $50 million running balance on ARF's cash operating account would yield another $250,000 a year as well as all of the potential accounts affiliated with ARF. I explained that the firm's negative press and our declining stock price had necessitated a change in strategy. In order to reach my production goals, my focus had shifted from the acquisition of traditional accounts to projects like ARF.

This may not have been a politically astute comment, but it was the truth. At this point, not even the most experienced financial advisors were bringing in new accounts by touting the trustworthiness of Merrill Lynch. The advisory side of Merrill Lynch was battening down the hatches, and Don Plaus knew it. I could tell he was ticked that I had assumed the authority to make such a big decision without consulting someone higher up the chain of command, but there was little he could say when I pointed out that at the heart of the issue was our responsibility to act in the client's best interests.

Don knew that I had made the right decision. He reserved comment on the second part of my explanation that involved my new strategy to make my goal, but I could tell having a greenhorn say this to him dinged his ego. It would have been much wiser to keep my big mouth shut because the second part didn't need to be said. Hindsight is twenty-twenty. Besides, when I said it, I was on a roll. It is a condition I suffer from frequently.

In the middle of August 2008, Emily and I learned through Derek that Mosh had a verbal agreement with several investors in India and parts of the Middle East to provide a 50 percent equity piece of the deal. Derek called me to arrange for $400 million to be deposited into an escrow account to be held at Merrill Lynch. Since Emily had been responsible for setting up the original account, naturally the task of setting up these escrow accounts fell to her. My job was to arrange for the safe investment of these funds in a manner that would earn us some money and make Don Plaus smile.

Emily attempted to move heaven and earth in order to meet our client's escrow account expectations. Don's interest in the project had mobilized the administrative vice presidents in Charlotte. Frank Frazer and Randy Dennis were on the phone in a firm-wide effort to set up these escrow accounts, which had the potential of earning the firm some nice profits.

We were dumbfounded that neither Merrill Lynch nor First Republic Bank, an entity recently purchased by Merrill Lynch on the West Coast, were not able to accommodate this seemingly mundane task. Emily noticed that First Republic even had escrow accounts advertised on the home page of their Web site.

Derek told us he expected most of the funds would be in $75 million increments and come via Bohemian banks. The international flavor of the transaction necessitated meeting Patriot Act requirements. Having the funds transferred into the accounts was seamless under the Patriot Act, but before funds could be dispersed, their origin had to be thoroughly documented.

ARF and Fontaine Capital were prudently requiring this condition be met prior to transferring the funds. Having done this previously, Mosh was concerned we were not asking the right questions and requesting protocol information.

About five days into the effort, Emily came to me with the incredible news that even with the muscle of Don Plaus's minions, Merrill Lynch was not going to be able to provide the escrow accounts. Although no one would admit the reasons, I suspect the failure of the auction rate securities market was preventing us from fulfilling our obligation to ARF. Don Plaus's vice presidents had no answer.

My insurance background kicked in, and I viewed this situation as a potential liability for the firm. In my mind, there was only one honorable thing to do. Confirming with Frank Frazer and Randy Dennis that Merrill Lynch was not going to be able to perform, I suggested we call BB&T Corporation, a leading regional bank with over $165 billion in assets headquartered in Winston-Salem, North Carolina. With some ambivalence, they agreed.

In the course of this communication, it was obvious that neither Emily nor the Charlotte contingent had ever considered pounding away at the problem until it was solved. The only context in which they could conceive of a solution was within their scope of influence. It was the limited way of thinking I mentioned earlier showing through again.

My approach to the problem was from the client's standpoint, which meant my point of view was entirely different from those trying to help me. I realized how much larger my perspective was than these industry veterans who had no practical experience outside of the financial services industry. At that moment I found myself in a culture that was different than I had originally perceived. This episode had uncovered the foundational attitude of my colleagues at Merrill Lynch, and it was shockingly self-serving for a supposedly client-focused organization.

One of my first social events in Blueberg had been a Friday morning Bible study held at the Blueberg Grill. There I was introduced to Stan Parker and Tom Ellers. Stan was the head of commercial lending for BB&T in Blueberg, and Tom was the city executive. These men projected an image of humility and enjoyed community-wide respect. It's hard to imagine two guys held in higher esteem than Stan and Tom. When in the course of human events it becomes necessary to swallow a big, beefy chunk of pride, these are the guys you want on the other end of the line.

Initially I called Tom, and after hearing my story, he referred me to Stan. Right from the start it became obvious we were dealing with true professionals. Stan put me in touch with the right people at BB&T, and they started asking the right questions.

After I spoke with the folks at BB&T, I knew for certain I had been dealing with bush leaguers at Merrill Lynch. Merrill Lynch had a platform second to none when it came to running money, but as a bank, Merrill Lynch was a joke. Both Emily and I wondered if the Total Merrill marketing campaign touting the vast platform of Merrill Lynch was a hoax and if our firm might be in terrible financial trouble. When you're working for a financial institution that is unable to accept $400 million, suspicions are aroused.

Embarrassingly, we did not have the answers to BB&T's questions, which centered on the number of investors at ARF. Records of investments must be reported to the IRS on K-1 reports that were sent to each participant. The ability to make money on the escrow account would be determined by the associated administrative cost. BB&T wanted to know about these issues and a few other housekeeping items.

Being novices, Emily and I thought we might be able to arrange a complete solution for ARF before making that dreaded phone call to Derek and Brock informing them that mighty Merrill could not handle a simple escrow account. We were looking for ways to couch this so it didn't look like Merrill Lynch was completely inept, but those hopes vanished in the realization that not only did we not know what we were doing, but apparently no one in our organization knew what they were doing, either. There was nothing left to do but pick up the phone and make the call to Brock and Derek.

Instead of making excuses, I simply regurgitated the facts as they were. I allowed Brock and Derek to draw their own conclusions about Merrill Lynch and quickly focused on the solution that BB&T would be able to offer. With hat in hand, we introduced our largest potential client to one of our competitors. Never in my wildest dreams could I have envisioned such a turn of events when I selected the almighty platform at Merrill Lynch upon which to build my career in the financial services industry.

The efficiency of the BB&T team was phenomenal. In the course of my experience, the only rival that came to mind was the book transition team that had invaded our office one year earlier to help Emily and Tom move from Smith Barney. When comparing the core competencies of each organization, one could only draw the conclusion that somewhere along the way Merrill Lynch had lost its track.

One organization was client-focused, and one was not. Even though this was my first experience with the Merrill Lynch Bank, these missteps were major. All this just did not add up, and I had to suspect that in the hallowed halls of Wall Street, the cornerstone was cracking.

8. Mister Big Stuff

Now because you wear all those fancy clothes
And have a big fine car,
do you think
I can afford to give you my love?
You think you're higher than every star above.

– Carrol Washington, Joe Broussard, and Ralph Williams

The chairmanship at Merrill Lynch of Earnest Stanley O'Neal was an absolute national disaster. Upon his appointment in 2003 as Merrill Lynch's CEO and chairman, he made his first order of business to declare war on the Mother Merrill culture that had generated the company's success through boom and bust for over eighty years.

His maniacal reign over the legendary Wall Street powerhouse began at the worst possible moment, both for the firm and for the nation. While his assessment of the culture dovetailed with the conclusions drawn in this book, his solutions and methods only exacerbated the cultural rot plaguing the organization and the financial services industry.

In an iron-fisted power play, he attempted to enforce his will with a supercilious attitude manufactured by the very beast he sought to kill. His conceit and defensiveness precluded him from understanding that only by adopting policies that fostered transparency could the culture be altered.

In an asinine strategy to purify the culture at Merrill Lynch, Stan O'Neal cultivated the fear of subordinates and dialed in the firm's goals, abandoning all measuring sticks except one: the return on equity at Goldman Sachs.

In direct defiance of retiring CEO David Komansky's edict to succession candidates to stay clear of the boardroom, O'Neal had openly campaigned for the CEO position. O'Neal lobbied the board of directors, expounding the virtues of reducing the bloated workforce at Merrill Lynch to increase the firm's return on equity (which was below that of its rivals on the Street).

The Merrill Lynch board of directors, mentally AWOL, appointed this man to head up the Thundering Herd even though he had never been a member of the herd. Asleep at the wheel, they failed to read between the lines of O'Neal's plan. "Bloated workforce," to people within the organization, was clear code for the Mother Merrill culture. Mother Merrill had come to represent a clubbish culture that enabled the wealthy to take care of their own. It was a culture in which brokers had come to expect the firm to watch their backs and act in the brokers' best interests at the expense of clients.

O'Neal detested the culture that he viewed as the main obstacle he had overcome in his ascent to the corner office. With an arrogance that belied a deep-seated insecurity, he set out to rid Merrill Lynch of what had made the firm financially successful. To be sure, Mother Merrill's culture was the epitome of the broker-first/client-second attitude, but O'Neal, having correctly diagnosed the aliment, inadvertently played into the hands of his critics and those he hated most. He failed to understand the nature of the beast he was riding.

Step one in his plan was to cut the broker support staff by 20 percent. This convinced the board that O'Neal was serious about increasing Merrill's return on equity, and the move was almost immediately beneficial to the stock price. The elimination of so many coworkers signaled to the rank and file that an autocratic bean counter was now running the show. What went undetected by the board, and by those buying the shares, was a fundamental shift in the organization's focus that would eventually bring down the lumbering Wall Street giant.

Increasing shareholder value over the short term and adhering to a prudent long-term strategy are almost always conflicting goals. Keeping in mind that Merrill Lynch's true clients are the brokers employed by the firm, O'Neal's staff reduction was a major deviation from policies of the past, and by proxy, the firm's clients suffered. The undetected element in this policy shift was a blind effort to increase shareholder value at all costs that, in the end, included a forty-to-one leveraging of the balance sheet.

Instead of building a leaner wealth management machine to meet client needs, O'Neal turned the focus of the firm away from the Thundering Herd and began an obsession with the investment banking operation. He believed the investment banking side of the house could implement his new business plan and earn profits to compete with Goldman Sachs. The brokers who weren't let go were doomed to play second fiddle during the O'Neal administration.

Using his autocratic muscle, he sought to marginalize the culture that had been created by the firm's tendency to placate brokers. To carry out his strategy, the influence of those on the other side of the power struggle had to be eliminated. The upper management team embraced the fallacy of betting the existence of Merrill Lynch on the ability of unemployed homeowners to make their mortgage payments.

O'Neal's vision of the future included the creation of an international cadre to lead Merrill Lynch, excluding anyone from the brokerage side of the business or anyone who might be a threat to his power base. His first pick was Arshad Zakaria, age forty, as executive vice president of Merrill Lynch & Co., Inc., and president of Global Markets and Investment Banking (GMI). Zakaria was a banking superstar from Bombay who constructed complex tax strategies and off-balance-sheet deals that ushered in the new regime and validated its direction for the firm. Zakaria had joined Merrill Lynch in 1987 as an investment banker.

O'Neal's closest confidant, and eventual co-president of the firm, was Egyptian Ahmass Fakahany, a former bean counter (a very accomplished bean counter, it must be noted) who had come over from Exxon some fifteen years earlier and progressed through the ranks. Although talented, he was young and possessed few credentials normally associated with such a position at a firm like Merrill Lynch. He met the most important criteria by not being a former broker or a threat to Stanley's power base.

Fakahany's co-president was Greg Fleming, who had been managing director of Global Investment Banking before his promotion. (Fleming would later save the firm from bankruptcy by engineering the Bank of America deal on a fateful weekend in September 2008.) He was neither a former broker nor a perceived threat.

Gone were the old guard of Kelly Martin and Mike Marks who had carried the water for brokers over the years. Martin at the executive committee level and Marks as the head of Merrill Lynch European, Middle Eastern and African operations, turned out to be irreplaceable.

O'Neal was not able to immediately eliminate all the old brokers from the ranks of the firm's decision makers. Australian James P. Gorman hung around until he was unceremoniously dumped in February of 2006. (In January 2010 Gorman became the president and chief executive at Morgan Stanley, a fact that must heap hot coals on the head of Stan O'Neal.)

Korean Dow Kim was hired to expand the CDO (collateralized debt obligations) market on the Merrill Lynch bond desk as the old guard was continually moved out along with their risk management acumen. This turned out to be one of Stan's most fateful appointments as Kim was charged with managing the firm's assumption of risk.

As he continually piled on risk at the urging of O'Neal, Kim felt the heat and left the firm holding a mortgage warehouse full of his incompetence. Stan O'Neal practically begged Kim to stay, which must have been a humbling experience for the autocrat struggling to remain tyrant. Kim's 2006 $35 million income made parting bittersweet. He launched a hedge fund that quickly closed when Stan O'Neal, ticked off because Kim's ill-timed departure left the CMO (collateralized mortgage obligation, a type of CDO) department in ruins, refused to invest in his fund.

As was standard practice for Wall Street CEOs, O'Neal reinforced his position of absolute power by populating the board of directors with easily manageable and inexperienced personalities at every opportunity. When the pot began to boil, O'Neal had solidified his power base; his removal should have come much earlier than it did. He was entrenched sufficiently to last until it became every man for himself. When the board fired Stan O'Neal, it did so because there was no other option.

In an overt attempt to extinguish the last vestiges of the old guard, O'Neal proudly instituted a strict policy of political correctness that permeated all decision making. The opportunity to establish a true meritocracy was lost to the pursuit of political correctness above all else. This new pervasiveness should have sent shivers down the spines of investors, but it went unnoticed or was applauded. O'Neal's misguided attempt to purge discrimination by edict was not only ineffective but was again symptomatic of the flawed mindset that eventually doomed the firm's balance sheet.

Instead of focusing on client needs, O'Neal indulged in the paranoid miscalculations that are typical of tyrants, and he poured salt in the wounds he had inflicted. On the day he was fired, Merrill Lynch's balance sheet was a steaming heap of dung, but the firm employed a workforce considered the most transgender-friendly in the United States. By voiding the organization of its competent old guard and placing politically correct yes-men in their stead, O'Neal managed to discard what was culturally beneficial from the days of Mother Merrill while simultaneously infusing the firm with an autocratic ethos that was anything but a meritocracy. Whether or not the workforce was friendly to the gender-challenged is not the point. The point is that for the stodgy Wall Street firm to have undergone such a change, management's influence and organizational recourses had to have been grossly misapplied.

The daily entrance and exit of Stanley O'Neal at Four World Financial Center, the Merrill Lynch headquarters in New York, was legendary. Upon his arrival by limousine in the parking facility located beneath the thirty floors occupied by the Merrill Lynch brain trust in lower Manhattan, Stan walked a short distance to his reserved elevator. With security guard in tow and whatever member of the inner circle had been granted face time with the supreme leader that morning, the self-important cabal ascended to the throne room. The entourage would be dismissed once Stan arrived at his perch atop Four World Financial Center to conduct the day's business. At the end of the day, he had an elevator reserved and waiting prior to his scheduled departure. In this way Stan O'Neal avoided having to interact with his lower minions and preserved his elitist disconnect with an arrogant style detested by practically everyone in the firm. If the elevators were slow to respond at the end of the day, everyone assumed Stan must be making his exit. This did not exactly endear him to those he was depending on to execute his remake of the firm.

The Merrill masses had their revenge. When Stan was in the heat of the battle to save his job, one of these disrespected employees found his USGA golf handicap calculation and posted it to the Web showing our fearless leader to be frequently on the golf course. If the perpetrator is reading this book, please accept my thanks and that of your beleaguered colleagues who labored in the wealth management division of Merrill Lynch across the nation at the time.

Stan O'Neal's autocratic hubris cleared the decks of anyone like Jeff Kronthal with the gumption to suggest that the firm might be taking on too much risk. Late to the mortgage game, O'Neal tried frantically to catch his nemesis, Goldman Sachs. The record is replete with accounts of Stan questioning his management team as to why Goldman Sachs had a greater return on equity than the Merrill Lynch balance sheet. He was myopically focused on beating Goldman Sachs to the exclusion of the firm's clients and more importantly the exorbitant risk-taking obscured by his greed.

This led to a series of horrific blunders that brought Merrill Lynch to its end.

Dow Kim was given the green light to leverage the corporate balance sheet in an effort to create and sell lucrative CDOs. In order to do this, Merrill Lynch needed a source of the odious high-coupon debt. Although they owned 20 percent of a small mortgage originator, this was not nearly enough debt to fuel an engine that would overtake Goldman Sachs. To remedy the lack of subprime debt, O'Neal decided to buy First Franklin, a purveyor of the lowest-grade debt in the system. They managed to buy this piece of junk at the top of the market.

When CDOs experienced a setback at the end of 2006 and the beginning of 2007, O'Neal's greed demanded that the firm journey down a blind path into a trap they sprung on themselves. In an effort to protect the firm, O'Neal's team demanded collateral from a couple of Bear Stearns's hedge funds that were having trouble making a payment on some CDOs. When the collateral was sent to Merrill's bond desk and the auction started, the bonds that were thought to be worth $1.00 drew bids of $0.65. With the advent of mark-to-market accounting, Merrill would have been forced to value many of the CDOs on their balance sheet at the sale price. They held off selling the bonds at this low rate, but the news got out and the damage was done.

By instituting the practice of warehousing this debt, O'Neal violated a long-held principle of Merrill Lynch. In the past, the firm had bought and sold before they bought again. Now they just bought and bought. To make matters worse, somewhere sitting in a corner on the other side of the trade was the dreaded Goldman Sachs. Judging that the market was simply progressing through a dip, Merrill Lynch allowed $60 billion worth of this junk to pile up on the balance sheet in short order. Stan and his boys were in too deep before they picked up on the fact that courtesy of Alan Greenspan's post-9/11 interest rate cuts, the U.S. housing market had been in a historic bubble, and the efforts to hedge their positions had been a farce. Stan O'Neal was caught in the middle of Wall Street with his pants around his ankles (I love that imagery). Anyone who had tried to head off this disaster had been summarily fired. I'm not sure what version of a meritocracy Stan O'Neal was shooting for, but it is safe to say he missed the mark.

The last straw for Stan O'Neal was a revelation that he had shopped our firm and its Thundering Herd to Wachovia behind the board's back. Once this became public, not even his lackeys on the board of directors could save his backside, and it became every man (or woman) for himself.

The brokers who had been paid their bonuses in company stock and owned a large percentage of the shares outstanding were outraged. Although the stock jumped 8.5 percent on the news of a possible merger with Wachovia, the revelation that O'Neal would have received $275 million if the deal had been done before those First Franklin chickens could come home to roost erased investor hopes. The market acted appropriately as the stock began its death spiral.

At the end of the day, the villainous Stan O'Neal, having wrecked one of the most prestigious investment houses in America, sailed into the sunset with the outrageous sum of $160 million in his pocket. It was not enough that he had fired 20 percent of the workforce and disassembled one of the most capable management teams on the Street. Stan O'Neal had almost single-handedly bankrupted Merrill Lynch. The lives and fortunes he destroyed along the way will not soon be forgotten, but his enduring legacy will be the central role his twisted administration of Merrill Lynch played in the socialization of the American economy and the systemic risk his pomposity inflicted on Main Street. Inside the firm, Stan O'Neal had a devastating effect on the culture. His drive to exceed Goldman Sachs's returns on equity increasingly misaligned the firm's goals with the interests of their clients and by extension the interests of its shareholders.

It would be unfair to place all of the blame for the failure of our financial infrastructure at the feet of Stan O'Neal, but on a sea of culpability, his ship certainly flies colors high and bold. He proved to be an unprincipled coward who, with $160 million in his pocket, walked away from the financial market mayhem he helped create. Only in America.

9. Flying Blind

Looking for a game, fortune and fame,
Waitin' just a little farther down the road somewhere.
Now Three Card Monty is a gamblin' game,
Two black aces and a pretty red queen,
Keep your eye on the lady and lay your money down,
Watch the fastest hand you've ever seen.

– Dickey Betts

I n late 2007, it was impossible to know the full extent of the economic con-
tractions that would birth the most ferocious financial crisis since the Great
Depression. What we financial advisors at Merrill Lynch did know was that
our brand had been forever tarnished. Merrill Lynch had endured past scandals,
but even at this early stage we knew this was on a different scale. Never before
had the chief executive officer brought such shame to our proud organization.

Jay Leno's jokes may have offended the egos inhabiting Four World Financial Center, but they were also beginning to erode our income in Blueberg. At
the time of Stan O'Neal's departure, the cracks in our brand were small and
maybe even repairable. Had the O'Neal episode ended on nothing more than a
sour note, the Thundering Herd would have stampeded back, but the damage
was too deep and too hidden.

In the midst of the chaos and unaware of the worthless assets on our balance sheet, the financial advisors at Merrill Lynch did achieve some vindication. The source of income from the fees and commissions earned by the FAs in Merrill Lynch offices worldwide had always commanded respect throughout the firm. The advent of the Internet and the $7 stock trade, coupled with the volumes of information available to investors online, struck at the heart of the traditional earning capacity of financial advisors and the financial services industry as a whole.

The industry's answer was twofold. On the financial services side of the house, the annuitization of assets began to be emphasized over transactional income. And, thanks to the repeal of the Glass-Steagall Act, investment bankers were able to earn enormous sums by using depositors' funds as collateral for loans. By leveraging up the balance sheet, these debt dealers became the income producers within the organization.

This was a hard pill to swallow for the echelons previously tasked with increasing shareholder value, namely the financial advisors. With the downfall of Earnest Stanley O'Neal, the world had been set back on its axis as the misplaced and ill-conceived bets of these careless debt dealers became known to the world and their hero status within the firm disappeared. These braggarts, who had been the underpinning of O'Neal, were now due an ample serving of humble pie, and the bosses in the wealth management division were all too happy to serve it up.

The board of directors at Merrill Lynch developed two qualified candidates to fill Stan's position. One was Larry Fink, head of BlackRock, one of the largest mutual fund companies in the world, 49 percent owned by Merrill Lynch. The other was John Thain, former head of the New York Stock Exchange and former member of the Goldman Sachs management team.

Larry Fink had the temerity to ask for a look at the company balance sheet before committing to the interviewing process. Mr. Fink, it seems, had a notion that things were pretty bad at Merrill Lynch, and trying to read tea leaves was not the way he planned to make his decision. Having suffered through his own turmoil in the early 1990s, Fink was not about to travel that road again.

The board suspected that given his bond expertise he might advocate a massive deleveraging of the firm's balance sheet. This would necessarily reveal that the assets now listed on that balance sheet, accumulated under the board's supposed supervision, were worth far less than what was being reflected on the quarterly earnings reports.

Fink was known as the conservative money manager who had profitably navigated troubled waters in his fixed-income shop at BlackRock. An evaluation with the scrutiny Fink had in mind would expose the board's mishandling of Stan O'Neal and Dow Kim's blind dash into $60 billion worth of subprime debt.

Larry Fink's intelligence and courage disqualified him for the position.

To center stage stepped a man who happened to bear a strong physical resemblance to Clark Kent, and who offered the prospect of a new day and a new beginning in which the army of financial advisors would once again rule the roost. John Thain was neither a coward nor stupid, but his outlook on the Merrill Lynch situation mirrored what the board was predisposed to believe, or what they hoped was true.

On November 14, 2007, the board appointed John A. Thain chairman and chief executive officer of Merrill Lynch, effective December 1.

While Thain set out to solve the mortgage delinquency problem, Bob McCann took a much higher profile in the organization. Almost overnight, the Thundering Herd had reclaimed management's focus, and McCann's job was to thwart any attempts by the competition to make inroads into the ranks of the organization's most valuable asset. From the perspective of financial advisors, a better day had dawned—or so it seemed.

The trouble with new days is that sometimes they come with very high mountains to climb. As the calendar ushered in 2008, the financial advisors at Merrill Lynch recognized the towering peaks on the horizon. The firm's share price had been cut in half from where it stood at beginning of 2007, when the gaudy income figures produced by the structured debt department had pushed the share price up to $93.

Wall Street rightfully wondered how difficult it would be for the Thundering Herd to replace the cash cow that was now hamburger. With the evaporation of Merrill Lynch's primary source of income, the share price dropped to $48.17 on January 8, 2008. But the notion that we might be rearranging furniture on the deck of one of Wall Street's several *Titanics* occurred to no one—certainly not to John Thain.

The collapse of Bear Stearns in March quickly evaporated any hope that the market was going to shake off its malaise and restore value to the exotic securitized debt instruments saddled with subprime lending practices. If Merrill Lynch was to survive, the firm had to convince investors that the income from wealth management operations would yield a sufficient return on equity.

There was no pretense that the days of 30 percent ROI were ever coming back, but Merrill Lynch was in need of some evidence of future growth potential. With renewed vigor, the structured products (not to be confused with structured debt) group continued to issue instruments with high commissions, neatly obscured in the prospectus. The 2 percent commission (on some products it was as high as 4 percent) split by the financial advisors and Merrill Lynch was paid in a fashion much more lucrative than a mutual fund.

There was an enormous difference between mutual funds and the structured products emanating from the ever-creative bowels of Merrill Lynch. Structured products had a maturity date, which meant that at some point in time (usually fourteen months), the vigilant financial advisor could roll those funds into a *new* product with a *new* 2 percent skim.

Besides their lucrative nature, another difference was that unlike mutual funds, which held shares of stock to secure their value, structured products were actually debt instruments. In a final assault on the victims of this risk switcheroo, structured products often came on paper backed by the likes of Merrill Lynch, Bear Stearns (until its early demise), and most prominently, our good friends at AIG.

On February 8 and 9, 2008, at the Westin Hotel in Charlotte, North Carolina, managers of the two regions headed up by Scott Hotham and Don Plaus (the South Atlantic and Southeast Coastal complexes respectively) held a combined quarterly sales meeting. The meeting consisted of presentations by Bob Doll of BlackRock and Mary Ann Bartels from our own commodity research staff, and they offered fairly upbeat forecasts for the coming year.

The meetings were held in the large ballroom over the course of two days, a Friday and Saturday. These appearances were also mixed with presentations from representatives of the mutual fund companies who had helped pay for the event, some high-priced motivational speakers, and members of management.

At this meeting, the delivery of the usual rah-rah speeches was eagerly anticipated because with all the upheaval everyone was interested (for once) in what the managers had to say. But there was an outlier on the agenda. The structured products division from New York was featuring as a speaker none other than Liam O'Neil, its managing director. Apparently this presentation was too important for one of the underlings from the sales desk. The topic of the talk was "Using Structured Products to Enhance Your Portfolio Returns and Your Business Model." That is code for "increasing the take of your client's assets without them noticing."

Promptly at one fifteen on Friday afternoon, when attendance was at its peak, Liam O'Neil began to expound on the virtues of purchasing a debt instrument with derivatives on the S&P 500 that would make a splendid substitution for a significant portion (if not all) of a client's large-cap portfolio allocation.

With a twinkle in his eye, Liam enthusiastically explained that at maturity in fourteen months, FAs could easily earn another 2 percent by rolling over the proceeds from these expiring notes into the latest incarnation of his cerebral structured-product aficionados in New York.

I was astounded that these debt instruments would be represented as having the same risk profile as a group of large-cap stock positions. The veracity of the notes was subject to considerable counterparty risk. In other words, if the firm that owed the investor was unable to pay, it mattered not that these notes would otherwise pay three times the return on the S&P 500's upside performance below 18 percent.

As a financial advisor at Merrill Lynch, I had no idea how much money the firm was earning on these products. I did know that the structured products team was deploying leverage to achieve these returns. How they were doing it was never sufficiently explained. The arithmetic in the prospectus was beyond my deciphering abilities, although, to my credit, I did sit down several times in an attempt to understand how and what these eggheads were doing.

When I asked Richard and Rudy about the particulars on some of these notes, they gave me the same song and dance clients received. When pressed for specific answers, they obviously understood these products less than I did. When I asked the salty old veteran Tom Hawkins, I loved his reply: "I don't understand 'em, so therefore I don't sell 'em." Immediately I assumed the Tom Hawkins position on structured products. If Tom Hawkins couldn't understand them, they couldn't be understood.

It was sometimes difficult to watch Rudy and Richard sell upwards of $7 million worth of a particular structured product issue and not participate in the windfall that came along with such an effort. For the mathematically challenged, 2 percent of $7 million is $140,000. Rudy and Richard pocketed around $60,000 on such campaigns. Not bad pay for three or four days spent calling through your client list targeting gullible souls unfortunate enough to be holding excess cash.

Hank Patton would proudly look on as Rudy and Richard banged out call after call, issue after issue. They were the compliance department's nightmare but management's knights in shining armor. After they left the firm and their shenanigans were revealed, I was disgusted by their methods and the wealth they had sucked from unsuspecting clients. What made it even more abhorrent is the wealth and privilege into which they, along with Hank Patton, were born and the callous disrespect they showed for those less fortunate. Sadly, they were the rule not the exception.

Quick to judge the supposed attitudes of entitlement held by those in poverty receiving government assistance, they were oblivious to their own intense feelings of entitlement to unearned bounty. They considered $60,000 for a week's work to be fees paid for services rendered.

The recipient of those services was considered to be Merrill Lynch, not the client. That, in a nutshell, is why this book is being written.

Richard and Rudy were just playing the dirty cards they had been dealt, and in their own minds they were doing an outstanding job. Merrill Lynch provided a quality spoon, and they used it to skim a layer of fat off their clients' money. Hank used to refer to them as "hired guns." It's a stark indictment of the wealth management culture that continues unabated today.

In spite of the optimism that came with Stan O'Neal's ouster, there were issues affecting the survival of the firm. There was no way the wealth management division could replace the income loss of the mortgage debt disaster. The wealth management division's drive to simply generate more income was merely an effort to exhibit a sustainable cash flow with some reasonable prospect for growth. The performance expectation was really no different than what it had been—only the spotlight was now focused intensely in the direction of the FAs.

As much as management wanted to believe differently, Stan O'Neal could never have succeeded in gaining control of the firm had there not been seeds of truth in his assessment of the Merrill Lynch culture. O'Neal lacked gratitude and humility, which blinded him to the fact that the culture he hated so intensely enabled his ascent to power. But he was on target with his contention that the ranks of the Thundering Herd were filled with undeserving, incompetent people who felt entitled simply because they perceived themselves as being at the top of the gene pool.

A living embodiment of Stan O'Neal's beef with Mother Merrill resided in the corner office of the Blueberg outpost in the person of one Ted Tiller.

10. Eminence Front

The drinks flow. People forget.
That big wheel spins, the hair thins. People forget.
Forget they're hiding. The news slows. People forget.
The shares crash, hopes are dashed. People forget.
Forget they're hiding. Behind an eminence front.
An eminence front—it's a put-on.

– Pete Townshend

Ted Tiller was a phenomenon of survival within Merrill Lynch. His father was an important early employee of the firm and responsible for much of its growth, but even that couldn't diminish the fact that Ted obviously had the luck of the Irish in his professional life. He must have had a leprechaun in his britches.

After coming to understand the depth of Tiller's incompetence, I was amazed his father had enough influence to perpetuate the son's career, but that seems to be what occurred. When I told people in Blueberg I worked for Merrill Lynch, the immediate reply was often, "Oh, so you work for Ted Tiller," which used to irritate me to no end.

I never failed to correct that insult, but there could be no mistake: in Blueberg, Ted Tiller was the face of Merrill Lynch. There was no question in my mind (and others later confirmed this) that news of Ted's mistakes was costing our office credibility and accounts. I was more affected by this fact than most of the FAs because it was my job to solicit new business.

But Ted's contribution to our declining credibility might have been remedied if only someone had taken him to task and demanded he be held accountable. But no one bothered. The problem was that everyone in the office was making money—good money—and therefore had no incentive to take the Ted Tiller bull by the horns.

Ted Tiller's self-centeredness knew no bounds. The first indication I got that Ted had issues came when he received a Christmas gift from his long-suffering assistant, Rikki Jakes.

One day while in Sam Reagan's office, I saw a decorative pewter plate with a number engraved on it. When I asked Sam about this object, he just smiled and said that the number was Ted's house number and that Rikki had given the plate to Ted for Christmas.

Sam explained that Ted had been incensed that Rikki would believe she had the necessary taste and discernment to select an object suitable for display at the fashionable Tiller residence located in the exclusive Black Forest neighborhood of Blueberg. It had never crossed his mind to politely accept the gift to spare Rikki's feelings.

Rikki earned about $50,000 a year. After bonuses, Ted reaped a minimum of $600,000 a year—more than ten times Rikki's pay.

How Sam came by the plate was never clear, but he and Rikki used it as a daily reminder of exactly who they were dealing with.

As Ted's partner, Sam Reagan was forced to deal with not only the other man's arrogance, but also with his incompetence. In my experience, the inconsiderate people I had worked with previously were required to have some modicum of competence to get away with being so self-absorbed. Not so at Merrill Lynch. In Ted's defense, he did not realize he was being inconsiderate, and he wasn't arrogant on purpose. Disregard for the feelings of lesser beings was just a symptom of his belief that his station in life was exalted.

Because sucking up to a certain class of folks was required to maintain his lifestyle, Ted was gentlemanly and polite in public. But if you did not inhabit that certain social class, you simply didn't matter to Ted. He felt some sympathy on occasion and dealt with the peasantry on an as-needed basis, but at the end of the day, if some peasant was getting screwed, it wasn't his fault or his problem. Ted worked tirelessly for local charities because it advanced his agenda of ingratiating himself to the people he wanted to impress.

Despite many well-designed strategies to navigate around Ted's issues, his partner never met with much success. There was the time, despite pleas to keep quiet, that Ted interrupted Sam's presentation to a prodigious investor concerning the significance of the emerging Asian markets. Ted felt compelled to interject that personally he was so convinced of the importance of these markets that even though his boys were in a Virginia prep school, he was making sure they learned to speak "Asian." As if that message weren't priceless enough, imagine the delivery in an accent reminiscent of former Sen. Fritz Hollings from South Carolina. And so it went time after time, episode after episode, in a daily assault on poor Sam Reagan's sanity.

As much as I hate to admit it, the burden Sam carried was an endless source of entertainment in the office, which gave me mildly perverse enjoyment. The following is an example of a lunchtime conversation with Ted.

Hal: Did you see Joe Biden on TV last night?

Ted: Who's Joe Biden?

Richard: You remember Joe Biden. He was a running back at UCLA.

Ted: Damn, Richard, you know I don't keep up with no damn football. I hunt and fish.

Hal: Well, last night on the *Jay Leno Show*, he took his clothes off.

Ted: What the hell did he do that for?

Reggie: He was trying to get gay people to send him money so he can run for president.

Ted: I ain't voting for his ass. Anybody that would take their clothes off on national TV ain't got nothing for me.

Reggie: Well, a lot of rich people support him, Ted, probably a lot of your clients.

Ted: What's his name again, Jim Bidden?

Richard: No, Ted, it's Joe Biden. He's the one dating Hillary Clinton.

Ted: I don't know how ya'll keep up with all that politics stuff. Who the hell cares who Hillary Clinton's dating?

Since his predictability made him an easy mark, Ted was constantly being toyed with. One instance stands out above all others. One day, Reggie purposefully allowed Ted to overhear what Ted thought was a private conversation that revealed that Herb Camp had just inherited $7 million.

Ted always felt that Herb's presence at Merrill Lynch was an indelible black mark on the office's social acceptability. The news that Herb Camp was walking a golden road into the social strata of Blueberg's elite curdled Ted's blood. Once

Ted found out about Herb's good fortune, he set out to confirm it with Hank Patton. Of course, Hank had been briefed and was prepared to add a little spice to the story by telling Ted it was his understanding that Herb had made an offer on the house next door to Ted's.

Ted's home in its prestigious neighborhood had been the focal point of his efforts to portray his affluence to those who mattered in Blueberg royalty. The prospect of Herb Camp as a next-door neighbor was a nightmare that stretched far beyond Ted's coping skills. The size and velocity of this calamitous shot from the outer reaches blasted a gaping hole in the fabric of Ted's life.

To make the devastation worse, Reggie and Sam arranged to have a local real estate developer drop by plans (strategically placed so Ted would accidently find them) which depicted a go-kart track (for Herb's two teenage sons) directly adjacent to the Tiller estate. Whenever the subject was broached, it brought a stutter to Ted's voice and caused sweat to bead on his brow.

A dastardly part of the torture of this con game was the constant on-again, off-again report that Herb's deal on the house was closing. If news came that the move was imminent, Ted would literally stumble to his desk to sit down in an effort to catch his breath. The ruse went on for months, and Ted's suffering was a constant source of hilarity. All the players were amazed at how superficial and immature a grown man could be in Ted's position as first vice president of investments at Merrill Lynch.

Towards me, Ted's attitude was at first ambivalent. Once he found out I cut my own grass, I fell into an office category Ted was able to manage. In his mind there were really only two types of people in the world: people who cut their own grass, and people of importance.

After I had been at Merrill Lynch for over a year, I bet Reggie lunch that Ted Tiller did not know my last name. I assumed we would then come up with a clever plan to find out.

But at that moment Ted walked out of his office. Reggie immediately said, in front of everyone in the bullpen, "Ted, do you know what Hal's last name is?"

"Sure I do," replied Ted.

"Well then, what is it?"

Ted paused and cocked his head like a robin listening for the faint sounds of the movement of earthworms. "Excuse me, I hear my phone ringing." He quickly retreated back to his office.

Reggie had to admit he'd lost that bet.

One spring day, in the ultimate display of superficiality, Ted found a use for me.

Sam Reagan and his wife, Kathleen, had sold their home in Black Forest and were living in a rental unit while they built a spacious new house on a rolling fifteen-acre site in a beautiful rural setting some ten miles out of town.

The exact location of the new house was not known to Ted. The only thing worse than having Herb Camp as a neighbor was the possibility of Sam Reagan, Ted's "inferior" partner, living in a home nicer than his own Black Forest abode. So as the home's construction neared completion, Ted and his wife, Susan, engineered a covert operation to learn the whereabouts of Sam and Kathleen's new house.

Ted had his chance when he heard me mention that I'd been out to Sam Reagan's new house.

Believing that I could lead him right to the scene, Ted kicked his plan into gear. After a hurried phone call to Susan, Ted announced to the office that she would be having lunch with us that day. In my time at Merrill Lynch, it was the only time she ever ate lunch with us. I thought that was unusual, but I still suspected nothing. To close the loop on the plan, Ted took Reggie's responsibility of selecting the eating establishment for the day's lunch by saying Susan was going to meet us at a barbecue joint ten miles out of town at a rural crossroads—conveniently located in the direction of Sam's new address.

On the long drive out to the restaurant, Ted nonchalantly suggested that since we were in the neighborhood, why not go by after lunch and see Sam's new house? After lunch I unguardedly guided the crew that consisted of Richard, Rudy, Reggie, Ted, Susan, and me to Sam's new property. As we walked up, Kathleen was busy unpacking boxes and setting up housekeeping in a beautiful new home. She was keenly aware of what was transpiring but was as charming and welcoming as always.

It was not until Sam (who had been absent from lunch) returned to the office and apprised me of the situation that I understood Ted had used me in his little scheme to spy on Sam. I apologized profusely and felt terrible about having let my guard down and about the imposition on Kathleen that resulted.

There are few things in this world more humiliating than having Ted Tiller get one over on you. I decided to believe he must have had Susan's help. I appreciated Sam's forgiveness and resolved to be less gullible. I never learned if Susan and Ted deemed Sam's new place competition, but I think they concluded it was far enough out of the city that any potential problem constituted a manageable situation.

We had to laugh at Ted to keep from crying. In the days of the declining Merrill Lynch share price, it became evident that Ted was taking it on the chin.

It was no secret in the office when he received a margin call, and as 2008 wore on, those calls were more and more frequent. It seemed Ted was resolving to do better. His pat comment was, "I've been living too high on the hog," an admission of what everyone in the office already knew. Three-hundred-and-fifty-dollar bottles of wine, drunkenly picking up expensive dinner tabs around town, and ever-increasing indebtedness were taking its toll.

Merrill Lynch management was aware of it, and everyone in the office was aware of it, but through unbelievable luck and an obsession with maintaining his appearance of affluence, Ted had managed to fool the public. Sam and Hank's efforts to conceal Ted's ineptitude had met with marginal success with the citizenry of Blueberg. I doubt anyone outside the firm suspected the gravity of Ted's situation.

From my insurance background, I did not understand how the firm tolerated the liability inherent in representing Ted Tiller as first vice president of investments in the Blueberg office of Merrill Lynch. The title insinuated he was competent enough to manage clients' assets. Although Hank and Sam had been running interference on Ted's behalf for years, their patience was wearing thin.

Bank of America had been trying to lure Sam away, and his efforts to use that as a bargaining chip with Merrill Lynch for still more perks and pay exposed Ted's true nature to management. But there is no better evidence of Merrill Lynch's true character than the blind eye management still turned toward Ted. The organization made a decision to ignore this broker's incompetence solely to protect a source of income for the company. Nowhere did the clients' interests and well-being figure into the equation. It was an equation that had no dollar sign next to the client variable.

As long as Sam and Hank were effectively covering Ted's backside, the fact that his clients were being shortchanged was of no concern to Merrill Lynch. Stan O'Neal's assessment of the culture that created many, many Ted Tillers within Merrill Lynch was in large measure accurate. O'Neal's sin was that he ingeniously found a way to make it worse.

11. Cauldron

Lights out tonight, trouble in the heartland
Got a head-on collision smashin' in my guts, man.
I'm caught in a cross fire that I don't understand.

– Bruce Springsteen

The world will never know if Larry Fink would have been able to save Merrill Lynch by jump-starting an immediate deleveraging of the firm's balance sheet. John Thain, stepping into position as CEO, believed the firm's survival had never been in doubt, even after Bear Stearns required rescuing when two of its hedge funds went belly-up.

Secretary of the Treasury Henry Paulson cajoled Jamie Dimon at J.P. Morgan into picking up the scraps for $2 a share (later revised to $10 a share) with some government financing and debt guarantees. This was the sugar that made the medicine go down, and the deal did well for Dimon. Seemingly unfazed, Thain issued the following statement at the bottom of Merrill's first-quarter 2008 earnings report:

> *Despite this quarter's loss, Merrill Lynch's underlying businesses*
> *produced solid results in a difficult market environment," said John*
> *A. Thain, chairman and chief executive officer. "The firm's $82 billion*
> *excess liquidity pool has increased from year-end levels, and we remain*

well capitalized. In addition, our global franchise is positioned strongly for the future, and we continue to invest in key growth areas and regions.

– Merrill Lynch First-Quarter Report 2008

That $82 billion in the bank was a great source of comfort to us on the front lines answering client questions while simultaneously searching for inner peace. Wholesalers coming through and pundits on CNBC assured us that the subprime problem was contained. A statistic heavily leaned upon was the minute percentage of the total mortgage market considered subprime.

We did not stop to consider that the low percentage of subprime debt to the overall mortgage market was due to the fact that Wall Street firms had been paying rating agencies to rate their new debt products. In this incestuous relationship, the quality of the ratings was directly related to the amount of fees paid to the underwriters of the debt.

It never occurred to us that the rating agencies might not have been doing their job. We did not know that AAA ratings were being handed out like candy at a six-year-old's birthday party, and I'm willing to wager investors in Norway, China, Brazil, and all places in between didn't know it either. Since it was the rating agencies' responsibility to designate subprime debt, and they were being paid not to designate it, this source of comfort, in retrospect, bordered on criminal.

Much to my discredit, I had no idea at the time how this process worked, but I was able to mimic to my clients what I was told about the low percentage of the debt that was subprime. You can bet your bottom dollar no one at Merrill Lynch was encouraging anyone to investigate the matter at the financial advisor level.

The one clue I did pick up on was the inverted yield curve, which I would have never seen were it not for Sam Reagan. When the first-quarter earnings report came out in April, I got a wake-up call.

To understand this wake-up call, some short background is necessary. After Stan O'Neal's disappearance into the sunset, speculation in the firm and on Wall Street was that the fourth-quarter 2007 earnings report for Merrill Lynch would reflect a housecleaning by the new CEO to rid the balance sheet of any questionable items that might hinder or reflect poorly on future earnings for which Thain would be responsible. For the year-end report to highlight everything that hinted of odor would be palatable, and given the number of O'Neal haters who had crawled out of the woodwork since his departure, Thain had a license to do what he considered necessary.

Suffice it to say he succeeded in shocking shareholders and financial advisors alike by reporting an almost $9 billion loss for 2007. The way we looked at it, this represented a tsunami that had wiped out the firm's efforts for the last two years. The report fueled anger at Stan O'Neal, but the rank and file were buoyed by management's proclamation that the worst was over. We were told there may be some "other shoes to drop" but that Thain had taken the necessary steps to right the ship. We had no reason not to believe what we were told.

When the 2008 first-quarter earnings report included a loss of $2 billion, the troops were not quite so understanding. The shoes that were dropping belonged to Paul Bunyan, and they smelled like he'd been walking around in Babe's stall. On our wealth management workstations, prior to the media conference call that would discuss the first-quarter earnings report, management communicated with FAs through the Merrill Lynch TV network. After our briefing, an announcement was made that regional director Don Plaus was going to host a conference call for his group to answer any questions.

I planned to ask him one of my own. In looking back at the year-end report, I found there was something I could not explain. On both the 2008 first-quarter report and the year-end 2007 report, the investment banking group was showing negative revenue.

I went to the deepest well of knowledge in the office on stock valuation, Tom Hawkins, and asked him to explain to me how writing down an asset on the balance sheet affected revenue. Tom was antiquated in some of his methods (he refused to carry a cell phone, for example), but when it came to this stuff, his thirty-two years in the industry came in handy. When he couldn't explain it to me, I felt better and worse at the same time.

My question had to do with the way I thought about assets versus income. To illustrate: if I were to learn that my beloved 1973 Ford tractor was only worth $3,000 instead of the $5,000 I paid for it, how would the amount of cash my wife could spend at the grocery store be affected?

At the risk of looking foolish, when Don asked if there were any questions, I spoke up. I said, "How does devaluing an asset on the balance sheet affect cash flow on the income statement? In other words, could you help me understand how we have a negative $2 billion revenue figure for the first quarter?"

Almost to my relief, he said that he did not know but that he would find out and get back to me. He never did, but that piece of information was invaluable. It was pretty clear to me that if Don Plaus didn't know how to read that earnings report, there were a lot of people making important decisions who didn't know what in tarnation was going on. Immediately I set out to educate myself.

The answer to my question was that the asset being written off was a stream of income that had been added to the income statement even though Merrill Lynch had not received the money. This is a common accounting procedure that I should have been intimately familiar with. The concept is taught in Accounting 101, and I am embarrassed to confess my ignorance.

Once I was reminded of this concept, the next logical question was how many of these chickens had we counted before they hatched? In other words, how much of our firm's income represented money that was owed to us but had little chance of being paid?

To me it seemed like a pretty straightforward question, but the answer was so complex that I could not understand it. There was no way to look at the documents provided under the SEC rules and determine much of anything. In retrospect, it is clear I was in a pretty crowded boat with John Thain as captain—and he didn't understand it either.

Meredith Whitney, the Oppenheimer analyst who was on top of all this, had the ability to go back through industry records and learn exactly who bought what and when it was packaged and sold. That is precisely what she did, and she made the information available to financial advisors like me who otherwise had no access to such facts or didn't know where to look for them.

The first quarter of 2008 had been my age of innocence. That period was over.

The noisy furor over the earnings report was short-lived. After all, no one wanted to be labeled as bearish on the firm. That would have been bad for business, and things were already challenging enough. We heard the reassuring platitudes we wanted to hear. Bright spots were Thain's importation of talent from Goldman Sachs and the return of the old guard, which was much preferred to the international politically correct cadre of the O'Neal administration.

There were, however, two dark clouds hovering over the economy, sending ominous signals to anyone paying attention. Sam Reagan's inverted yield curve had flattened but refused to steepen despite emergency rate cuts of historic proportions by the Federal Reserve. The second signal was the unmistakable sound of air escaping from the real estate bubble.

But in spite of the disastrous first-quarter earnings report, Merrill Lynch's share price was up from the first of the year. According to management, all was right with the world although there might be another "shoe to drop." Management poured the cyanide-laced Kool-Aid, and all of us financial advisors drank it down eagerly. I am not sure if it was because we wanted to believe what we were hearing or if we had just not taken the time to investigate the true nature of our plight. I suspect both were involved, but it was more the latter than the former.

The second-quarter earnings report was the catalyst that renewed my personal drive to understand what was going on within the firm. Shortly after the market had time to digest the first-quarter earnings report, the Merrill Lynch share price went into a free fall as the insiders on Wall Street began to suspect trouble. On May 2, the share price was $52.71, but on July 15, right before the second-quarter earnings report, the shares had plummeted to $24.69.

The second-quarter earnings report was completely different than what Thain had led us to believe it would be. The $4.6 billion loss left only two possible explanations for the false information we had been given by management. The first was that we were intentionally being lied to; the second was that management was clueless. I chose to believe that management, for whatever reason, had not accurately assessed the firm's exposure to toxic assets.

My inclinations were confirmed shortly after the second-quarter earnings announcement when Thain announced he was selling $31 billion worth of debt to Lone Star, a distressed debt purchaser of some renown in Texas. What caught my eye were the terms Merrill Lynch had negotiated. Not only had we sold the debt for twenty-two cents on the dollar, but Merrill Lynch had financed 75 percent of the purchase. When I read the announcement, I could hardly wrap my mind around the numbers involved and the implications of such a dramatic move.

One possible mitigating factor might have been Merrill Lynch's participation in eventual collection of the debt in excess of the twenty-two cents. Theoretically, the firm could have been handing off this bad debt to let Lone Star apply their expertise in debt collection to the $31 billion. Since we financed the purchase, logically Merrill Lynch might have negotiated a way to get more money out of the deal if the debt turned out to be worth more than the $6.7 billion selling price. Put simply, there should have been a way for Merrill Lynch to participate in the upside as compensation for making what appeared to be such a one-sided, sweetheart deal for Lone Star.

The other possible scenario was that Thain was making a desperate attempt to deleverage the balance sheet at any cost and in a hurry that bordered on panic. We all had to suspect the latter since we had sold off our Bloomberg stake just a few days earlier. As we gathered in the conference room to listen to another conference call from Don Plaus, I found myself with another question.

Asking a question on a conference call when all the experienced FAs and high-income earners were present was a little unnerving and I really did not want to be the one to speak up. As the question-and-answer period wound to a close, however, my issue had not been addressed, and I was not going to let it slide. Taking a deep breath, I asked, "Don, do we have any upside in this deal?"

His answer was quick and short. "No, we don't, Hal." Out of the hundred and fifty FAs on the call, he had recognized my voice. I was hoping to slip in under the radar. The way he answered the question, though, let me know that my question had been his question. This was bad news, but soon it was to be followed up by worse news. Looking back on it, I think Don knew what was coming down the pipe as he conducted that call.

Merrill Lynch announced the disaster of the firm's 2008 second-quarter earnings on July 17, followed closely by the Lone Star news, but the coup de grâce was the announcement on July 28 of the need to raise $8.5 billion in capital by diluting the company's shares. It was raining shoes.

The share dilution was a surprise step that had implications beyond what is normally associated with such dire news. The financial advisors' bonuses had been paid largely in company stock, and the high-earning producers within the firm were livid that they were taking an unexpected haircut on top of dealing with all the bad press day in and day out. The firm's most valuable assets were these big producers, and any move jeopardizing the firm's relationship with the crème de la crème of the Thundering Herd was perceived as being delivered by a hooded dude sporting a sickle in one hand. This indeed was the event that encouraged even the old bulls at Merrill Lynch to start taking those calls from headhunters as the buzzards began to circle.

It was in this tense, uncertain environment that I made an honest mistake that would reveal to me another key component and characteristic of the financial industry's fear-based culture. On the morning of July 28, with the announcement of the stock dilution, I ventured into the sanctum of Rudy and Richard's office to learn their reaction to the news. I thought they might have some insight as to why Merrill Lynch would pay Temasek Holdings a premium to issue the shares at $22.50. I wondered if there could be another explanation other than an emergency attempt to raise capital.

These brokers, each with twenty years' experience, did not care what this particular batch of tea leaves may have indicated about the future viability of Merrill Lynch. They simply knew that the value of the shares they had received upon their exodus from Smith Barney had just been reduced considerably. Rudy was visibly upset, so much so that the melody in his voice had turned into a dirge.

As the day wore on, I was very surprised no one from management had made any effort to explain the reasoning behind the decision to issue new shares. Hank Patton was at home with a severe back strain and had left instructions that he was not to be disturbed. As the atmosphere in the office began to deteriorate, I knew that management was unaware of what was transpiring in Blueberg. I made a decision to show some leadership and take action.

The progress on the $800 million ARF deal as well as another $20 million opportunity kept me in frequent contact with Don Plaus. I viewed Don as a resource in addition to being my boss. My past experience managing businesses taught me that a manager's first priority is to make sure employees have the tools necessary to complete their assignments. The other financial advisors in the office construed the relationship as being entirely and strictly a quid pro quo arrangement. There was no sense among other FAs that the organizational goals were worthy of any sacrifice on their part. From their perspective, Merrill Lynch retained a portion of the revenue they generated in return for services rendered. The financial advisors ran a business that paid Merrill Lynch for use of their platform, and their interest ended at that point. In their view, there was no situation that could not be made worse by the involvement of management. Although I knew these guys were afraid of Don, I did not understand the animosity that existed in the relationship.

I sent Don an e-mail giving him a heads-up that Hank Patton was not in the office and that in this current storm Merrill Lynch Blueberg was a rudderless ship taking in water.

Almost as an afterthought, I indicated he might want to reach out to Richard and Rudy since they had taken the dilution of the shares so hard.

Don immediately called Richard and Rudy to make sure they were not planning to do something rash. I am sure in the back of Don's mind was the fact that more ruthless structured product campaigns were going to be needed now more than ever.

Richard and Rudy did not perceive this as an indication of their importance to the Blueberg office, but rather an intrusion by management into their pity party. They immediately began to survey the office to discover who had ratted them out.

Immediately after he hung up the phone with Richard and Rudy, Don called Hank Patton's assistant, Elaine Massey, to find out Hank's status. Don had been sending e-mails all morning, which he assumed Hank was reading. (Don did not know that Hank had no idea how to check his e-mail.) When he learned that Hank was not going to be in at all that day, an announcement was made that at two o'clock there would be a conference call in the conference room and that everyone in the office was expected to attend. Don opened the call by thanking me for sending him the e-mail. Mystery solved for Richard and Rudy.

Immediately after the conference call, I left for a meeting in Atlanta and was gone for two days. When I returned, Hank called me into his office to get my side of the story. After I recounted what had happened that day and why I did what I did, the thought occurred to me that the leadership I had displayed in that moment of crisis might be a feather in my cap. Hank, Richard, and Rudy had a completely different take on what had transpired. In their eyes, I had labeled Richard and Rudy as malcontents and the instigators of office morale problems and had portrayed them as such to higher management.

In an effort to explain and make an apology, I immediately left Hank's office to find Rudy and Richard. They were not inclined to accept and were acting like third graders. One thing I've learned about elitists is they cherish any opportunity to portray themselves as victims. Living a life viewed by others as privileged makes the chance to shed the moniker, even briefly, irresistible. The duo had spent the previous two days bemoaning the viciousness of my act.

I never did find out what motives were ascribed to me. Nevertheless, I offered to forward them the e-mail I had sent to Don. Once they read the e-mail, they had to admit their conclusions had been wrong, but they still were unwilling to admit what I had done was an act of responsibility. I believe their victimhood masked bruised egos, and they were envious because they had not shown leadership in that moment. The fact that I was a greenhorn made my transgression all the more unacceptable and fueled the justification for their anger. Richard even had the unmitigated nerve to accuse me of throwing Hank under the bus, which was utterly ridiculous.

Contemplating what had happened and the reactions of the different players, I had to conclude that these guys were extremely immature and insecure. The degree to which the incident was blown out of proportion and all the dramatic rhetoric exposed their thought processes in ways I'm sure they did not understand. The experience reaffirmed my philosophy of "never let 'em see you sweat" because I had just witnessed how unflattering it can be.

Don Plaus genuinely appreciated what I had done, and that is what mattered to me. He was unaware of the persecution coming my way, but I had decided to let the matter drop. There was no time for bickering. Richard and Rudy calmed down after a while, but the office's atmosphere was different from that point on. I was henceforth regarded as Don Plaus's spy.

12. The Prediction

When I think back on all the crap I learned in high school,
It's a wonder I can think at all.
And though my lack of education hasn't hurt me none,
I can read the writing on the wall.

– Paul Simon

In an effort to calm the natives, on the first Tuesday in August Don Plaus made a trip to Blueberg to have a little face time with everyone in the office. As lunchtime rolled around, he invited all of the financial advisors to walk over to Margret's Restaurant.

As we finished our meal, Don started to his left and went around the table, asking each financial advisor whether, in their view, at the end of the year the market would be up or down.

As the twelve FAs sat around this table, the ultimate question had been put to them. Their answer would encapsulate their interpretation of the events that had transpired to bring us all together at that moment. Was this the market bottom, or was this just a stop on the way down?

The facts to be weighed included:

- Stan O'Neal had been fired;
- A former Goldman Sachs executive had been hired in his place;
- Merrill Lynch had reported an $8.9 billion loss for the previous year;
- Bear Stearns had capitulated when two of their hedge funds imploded;
- Our firm had reported multibillion-dollar losses in the first two quarters of the year;
- The Federal Reserve had embarked on a historic rate-reduction campaign;
- The U.S. Treasury had been forced, for all intents and purposes, to absorb Fannie Mae and Freddie Mac;
- Our firm had to offload $30 billion of bad debt;
- The FAs' share price was being diluted after frequent assurances by our new CEO that our capital position was strong.

These were just the lowlights of a torturous preceding twelve months. As each FA in turn answered the question, the sentiment was nearly unanimous: except for the newest member of the team, Nick Neapolitan, who had less than a year's experience, all the FAs expressed the firm belief that at year's end the market would be higher.

Sitting to my right was Emily Smith. After she gave the market her thumbs-up, it was my turn. I looked around the table, then straight at Don, and predicted that not only would the market be down, but something would happen before the election that none of us at this table could contemplate. Emily asked if I was predicting a terrorist attack. I repeated my description of what I foresaw as something we could not contemplate.

To my left, Hank Patton was last to record his prediction, and he quickly spoke up to squash any further discussion of my answer.

As I look back on those FAs making confident predictions in the face of dire events, I believe one of two sentiments must have guided them. Possibly they perceived a prediction of an up market as the answer Don wanted to hear. There was no elaboration with the exception of my comment. The responses had come out in one-word proclamations: "Up." This was the type of cultural dynamic that newcomers like Nick and I didn't know about.

The other possibility is that they viewed the magnitude of recent events as a sure bottom. As absurd as this point of view seems in retrospect, investors were in agreement with our FAs that day. The financials spurred the market to move higher.

I thought Don wanted an honest answer, so I provided one. In addition to the events that had already happened, there were ominous forecasts from some of the most esteemed analysts on the Street. David Einhorn's published speech, widely calling into question Lehman Brothers' attempt to hide in a footnote on its first-quarter earnings report admitting to a $5.9 billion CDO debt, was credible. Meredith Whitney was receiving death threats for saying Citigroup was bankrupt, which only meant that she was right about something. Although the boys at PIMCO were perceived as perma-bears, in addition to their usual refrain, they now were citing data points with concrete relevance.

All these analysts were esteemed, but the irrefutable logic of David Rosenberg, head of North American research at Merrill Lynch, was having the most influence on my thinking. All these guys were ringing the bell as loudly as it could be rung. To me, the trend that had started with deterioration in the residential mortgage market was continuing unabated.

Extrapolating a serious deflation in home prices was a frightening exercise. The Great Depression was due to a residential real estate price deflation brought on by the stock market crash of 1929. The only indicator that the worst had passed was the propaganda being bellowed by our management team and others with a vested interest in being bullish. Even the most ardent reassurances carried the ever-present caveat that there might be more problems round the bend, or some version of that warning.

In reality, the whole sorry series of events was starting to gather greater momentum, as evidenced by news so bad the election was starting to get bumped from the headlines. As more and more indications arose daily that events were spinning out of control, it became evident that no one, John Thain included, knew where this thing was going to end. Federal Reserve Board chairman Ben Bernanke expressed concern about inflation due to the emergency rate cuts made necessary by the Bear Stearns failure. Although unable to see the whole field, CNBC's Jim Cramer, whose hubris never ceases to amaze me, was screaming through the TV that the Fed knew nothing. The truth is that the Fed knew a lot more than Jim Cramer; they just didn't know how to interpret this new stage show in the financial markets. But give Jim Cramer credit. He was right to shout down Bernanke's inflation warnings in the midst of a crashing real estate market.

His thunder-bust notwithstanding, Jim Cramer does deserve credit for sounding a warning, but in mid-August of 2008 he had no more idea this was a systemic event than did Ben Bernanke. For my part, I was not using some deep mathematical analysis to come up with my forecast—it just seemed to me, as a down-home boy from Folksy, that whatever these smart guys were looking at, they had never seen it before, and they certainly weren't sharing the details with Merrill Lynch financial advisors.

Over the month of August, in the daily lunch-table debates I became a vociferous bear. Research and the media provided ample evidence to support my point of view, and although they would never admit it, my colleagues showed signs of being persuaded. Several FAs began to admit they were putting their personal investments into much more conservative allocations, and some, like me, were liquidating their investments and going to cash.

As financial advisors, we were struggling to understand the depth and breadth of what was upon us. We had been trained, as indeed the whole industry had been trained, to better advise our clients by identifying the appropriate stage of the business cycle.

Personally, I became obsessed with understanding Sam Reagan's yield curve, Fed rate policy, and the basis for what David Rosenberg was saying about the economy. While I had followed stocks all my adult life and knew how to evaluate equities, in April 2008 my bond IQ was embarrassingly low and would have to be improved dramatically if I was going to fulfill my obligation to my clients. If I had paid more attention to David Einhorn and what he was saying about the bond kings over at Lehman Brothers, my learning curve would have been shortened considerably. *C'est la vie.*

That August, partly because the golf course at the Blueberg Country Club had been closed since March for renovations, my spare time had been spent immersing myself in this mystery. During the last weekend of August my wife's brother was getting married in California so we headed out to San Francisco for that Labor Day weekend show. Having two teenage daughters who had never seen Yosemite, we decided to extend our stay to see the sights.

After going up to the overlook to view the majestic Half Dome, we started down the mountain in search of the great sequoias. As the girls chatted, I drove and thought about what element of the formula was missing. The more I considered, the more I knew there was indeed something missing in my understanding.

Unlike other times when I'd researched the data and studied the sequence of events, I was not at my computer screen. I was viewing the awe-inspiring gifts of God's creation. The natural beauty of the coniferous giants and the surreal views has a way of refreshing and clearing one's mind.

In this setting, I had to take a step back and examine the economic landscape holistically instead of analyzing a single data point or that day's headline. It was there and from that perspective that I was able to discern the key to unlocking the box that contained the missing piece of the puzzle.

The thought process started with a musing about what John Thain would love to say publicly but was unable to because of the situation on the ground. Every explanation and promise made to the financial advisors at Merrill Lynch by the leadership had carried the caveat that there might be other "shoes to drop," an explanation on which the leadership steadfastly refused to elaborate. Then I thought about what Ben Bernanke would like to say but could not, for he knew history was recording his every word.

My thoughts turned to Hank Paulson. The answer for all three was the same. I envisioned all three standing at a press conference proclaiming that whatever was occurring in the markets did not represent under any circumstances a systemic threat to our financial system or economy. How beneficial would such a blanket reassurance be to the economy and world markets? It would have been the golden statement. If these men could have categorically made such assurances and not been excoriated by history, they would have surely been participating in the mother of all media blitzes to cut off any possible panic.

Their extended silences and the obviously crafted public statements began to reveal an image like one of those multicolored creations that, when stared at long enough, yields a clear 3-D image from the mesh of slightly different colored dots. What was going on behind the scenes was an unscripted patchwork attempt by Paulson and Bernanke to stick fingers in the dike of a cascading systemic breakdown of the economy, and they were fast running out of hands.

As I thought more about the conclusions I was beginning to draw from this new idea of analyzing what was not being said, another important realization emerged to confirm what I was thinking. If this were indeed some type of systemic event, the confusion that was besetting policymakers would be logical and would provide perfect context for all the steps that had been taken thus far to avert disaster.

In October 1929, the last systemic event manifested itself with the crash of the stock market, but the economy did not cascade out of control until nearly thirteen months later when panic began to instigate runs on the banks around the country. Obviously none of the current policymakers had witnessed those events, and even though they may have studied the causes and actions of that era, there was no way to enter the emotions of the bygone time and accurately compare them with the present. This would surely account for all the confusion currently plaguing the leadership in our government and economy.

Many of the CEOs on Wall Street, and indeed the industry as a whole, had been steeped in the art of identifying different phases of the business cycle. It was the way people in this business got rich. A systemic event would have been impossible to recognize in a culture so singularly focused on viewing events through the lens of their experience and then developing an investment strategy to take advantage of an accurate forecast. A cataclysmic systemic scenario is the only explanation that left no aspect of recent events unexplained.

My first impulse was to call Sam Reagan, but with my sporadic cell phone service in the hills of Northern California, calling was impossible. So my train of thought shifted to attempting to identify what the next falling domino would look like if my conclusions were correct.

With this, I immediately saw a stark truth I had not yet considered. Even if the top brass and the smartest guys at the top of the firm's food chain came (or more likely had already come) to the conclusion that this was a systemic episode, they were powerless to help the financial advisors protect the firm's clients. After all, what had led to these conclusions was an examination of what John Thain and others were *not* saying. The revelation hit me that even if John Thain saw economic Armageddon on the horizon, there was no possibility on God's green earth that he was going to implore the firm's clients to get their houses in order (which is code a financial advisor would immediately recognize as a call for clients to start holding cash).

Merrill Lynch had in the neighborhood of $2 trillion under management, and a rush to sell such an astronomical amount of investments would have undoubtedly crashed world markets. It became clear that "too big to fail" was also "too big to tell." The bad news would have to be kept under wraps. As a financial advisor, I was largely on my own (although there was always David Rosenberg). Merrill Lynch had always touted the size of the firm as an attribute offering security to investors, but it was now the one aspect of the firm that made sounding the alarm impossible. The irony made me ill. At the most crucial time in the advisor/client relationship, the drama of a systemic event had left Merrill Lynch and all the other wirehouses helpless. When their clients needed them most, the industry was tongue-tied and handcuffed.

Before recommending decisive actions to my clients, my task was to indentify markers and signposts that would either confirm or deny all of these paranoid conclusions. I did have a leg up, along with Emily and Tom, in assessing just how dire our situation at Merrill Lynch had become. As I mentioned previously, our efforts to set up an escrow account on behalf of Ag Renewable Fuels had mysteriously been fruitless. To this day I do not know why Merrill Lynch could not accept $400 million. I can only assume that there might have been some administrative liquidity demand in exchanging the currency. That is the only explanation I can imagine, and it is purely a guess. The fact that Emily and I were not given an explanation was an alarming but extremely helpful backdrop to my thought process in California. In fairness to the other financial advisors, they did not have this look over the fence into the other side of the firm. The unexplained inability to set up these routine accounts was very disturbing. A systemic event would surely be preceded by some occurrences that made no sense and were unexplained by people with something to hide—occurrences like the inability to set up escrow accounts.

Another obscuring characteristic that would prevent detection of a systemic event in its infancy is the sheer outrageousness of such speculation. It is the stuff of Hollywood fantasy and special effects. The ruinous result of what would surely come to pass should the developments of the last half of 2007 and the first half of 2008 be extrapolated into the fall of 2008 seemed like science fiction. Few realized the implications of a calamitous collapse of the U.S. banking system.

Our financial system and economy is funded by a fractional banking system that is entirely dependent upon the confidence of depositors. If all depositors simultaneously sought to withdraw their deposits, the banking system would fail. On September 19, 2008, the Federal Reserve took drastic measures to prevent a crisis of confidence by guaranteeing money market funds deposited prior to this date. This announcement by the Federal Reserve can only lead one to assume that the specter of a collapse had the Federal Reserve Board shaking in their boots.

When policymakers used statements like "stand on the precipice" or "look into the abyss," they were seeking to avoid describing what would probably happen should the banking system fail. Imagine the scene inside retail stores if customers' debit and credit cards were mysteriously denied without warning or explanation. The chaos that would ensue when families and businesses were suddenly denied purchasing power would threaten the very fabric of our society and the rule of law. A society so suddenly robbed of currency is without precedent because of the electronic nature of our modern banking system. Never before could a nation (and probably the world) be deprived of purchasing power at the speed of light. At that point it would become every man for himself, and the run on the bank would turn into a run on the supermarket.

That is what the abyss looks like, and that is exactly where we were, and may still be, headed. As an amateur historian, I also know that in the course of human history such economic crises often create a societal imbalance that only finds equilibrium on a battlefield.

These dire consequences would only occur after a run on the banks, which gave me some comfort until I stopped to consider what a modern-day run on the bank would look like. Previously my only mental picture of these circumstances had been gleaned from history textbooks and the movie *It's a Wonderful Life*. In contrast, a modern run on the bank would look much different. When I thought about the freezing-up of the auction rate securities market, the failure of Bear Stearns, the fate of Freddie Mac and Fannie Mae, and all of the issues with Merrill Lynch and the escrow accounts, I had a new vision of a run on the bank, and it was happening now. This was it, a financial crisis of the first order, a moment in history that would be studied by my children and their children.

The fact that making such statements invites labels of "alarmist," "paranoid," "crazy," or "unstable" does not make the predictions less likely to happen. On the contrary, no one, especially a still-wet-behind-the-ears FA, wants to stand up and yell "fire!" in a crowded theater. I had to be careful of the company in which these unspeakable subjects were discussed. As I thought about these issues, I could only describe the situation as a massive, unprecedented deleveraging of the economy—a modern-day run on the bank.

Upon my return to Blueberg, I stepped past the fountain out front at a brisk pace, into the Merrill Lynch enclave, and straight into Reggie Sparks's office where he and Sam were strategizing. As I began to explain what I had come to see so clearly, my excitement characteristically included my habit of hand movements to punctuate my conversation. The source of endless ribbing, the hand movements that naturally accompany my pontifications had been a favorite needle of Reggie Sparks, which on other occasions I took good-naturedly. This morning I was in no mood for the immature office jib jab.

Emphasizing repeatedly that the sequence of events we had been analyzing were not part of the business cycle but rather a systemic episode leading us into the abyss was a frustrating exercise. As I tried to ignore Reggie's mocking hand motions and Sam's adherence to the business cycle, I could see that I was making no headway. Every counter to my argument was an incredible adherence to the business cycle lens of viewing the whole affair. When Reggie Sparks refused to lay off the hand motion mimics, I became angry and walked back to my office determined to let them roast, along with their clients.

Sam shortly followed to ask if I was really convinced of what I was saying. I told him again in the strongest terms possible that if he continued to view the economic developments as a normal prelude to a run-of-the-mill recession, then there was little chance of him or anyone else being able to understand the gravity of the situation. We ended the conversation agreeing to disagree, which gave me cause to doubt my conclusions and seek further confirmation.

It was not long in coming.

13. Conviction to Act

Looking out at the road rushing under my wheels,
I don't know how to tell you all just how crazy this life feels.
I look around for the friends that I used to turn to, to pull me through.
Looking into their eyes, I see them running, too.

– Jackson Browne

On September 12, 2008, I was having my weekly Friday afternoon conversation with Coach Ford, and after going over a couple of items he asked me, "Well, buddy, what do you think is going to happen?"

Jokingly I replied, "Monday morning I'll probably be working for Bank of America."

It was a statement based on pure speculation and was meant to indicate to Coach anything was possible in this crazy market. The vibes were there and something was surely afoot, but I meant the comment to be a joke.

Considering in retrospect what was taking place behind the scenes on Wall Street, it is clear the investing public, as a whole, was thrown under the bus by their too-big-to-fail, too-big-to-tell wealth management firms. These firms had no choice but keep their financial advisors in the dark about the troubles that faced the economy and their firms.

Never before had the true nature of the relationship between management and the financial advisors been so openly adversarial. By Sunday afternoon of September 14, Merrill Lynch management was not only frantically trying to help Bank of America complete its due diligence, but there was a concerted effort to spin the Monday morning news in an effort to keep the Thundering Herd from stampeding out of the door. Although John Thain's decisive action of selling the bad debt to Lone Star made a deal with Bank of America possible and avoided the result Lehman Brothers endured, Thain's bumbling misstatements had cost him credibility.

The task of holding intact the firm's last most valuable asset, the financial advisors, fell to Bob McCann. Popular with the advisors and from the retail side of the business, McCann had the only voice with enough credibility to stem a mass exodus. An evacuation of financial advisors to the competition would torpedo the consummation of any deal with Bank of America. Ken Lewis, president of Bank of America, had coveted the reach of sixteen thousand aggressive sales associates and had made a deal over the course of the weekend that would typically take months and months of negotiations to close. With Hank Paulson's urging, cooperation, and eternal gratitude, Ken Lewis and John Thain (actually, it was Greg Fleming, president of Merrill Lynch) had engineered a deal to save the Bull. But the markets rightfully remained unimpressed, and the week to come was one for the books on Wall Street.

Monday morning's news of the Bank of America/Merrill Lynch announcement left the Blueberg office in shock. We had all the standard communications from management, and the internal Merrill Lynch spin machine was spitting out what everyone expected. Our announcement coupled with the Lehman bankruptcy news precipitated a breathtaking 504-point drop of the Dow Jones Industrial Average. All day long financial advisors fielded calls from clients and in turn tried to put our best spin on the stunning turn of events. Fielding questions started out as a mission to calm the nerves of jittery clients but soon turned into a humiliating experience.

The truth of the matter is that, although we had better context, our understanding of specifically why this had happened and its implications was not much greater than our clients. We had no meaningful direction to offer as the calls continued to pour in. A distracted management team was concentrating on the merger details, babysitting the firm's big producers, and reaching out to institutional investors. Retail clients were far down management's priority list. Their focus was not on the financial advisors' clients but rather on the firm's clients, the big income producers who populated the Thundering Herd.

Ignoring the firm's retail investor clients, management's focus was to develop strategies to placate the heavy hitters in the retail and private banking ranks. In those dark hours at Four World Financial Center, preventing an FA hemorrhage across the country was paramount. My quest to identify actions that would support my theory of an impending systemic crisis ended that day, but it was no thanks to any information distributed by the Merrill Lynch management team. After Monday, September 15, in my mind there were no unanswered questions as to the seriousness of the situation. Any remaining doubt that the situation had spun out of control had been eliminated.

On Tuesday, to everyone's relief the market rebounded slightly, only to sink Wednesday in a 684-point plunge that beat the Monday panic. The market was being introduced to a level of volatility that had never before been witnessed. One day the Dow was up 900 points; the next day it was down 500. As confused as everyone was, and given the incredible lack of direction provided by management, financial advisors like me were left to fend for ourselves and our clients.

In the morass of opinions, anecdotal stories, and analysts' contradictory interpretations, there were two facts I decided were irrefutable and worthy to act as the foundation of my recommendations going forward.

The first was that the markets were not functioning correctly. Sitting here today writing this that sounds like the understatement of the millennium, but at the time the conclusion was fairly radical. The wild swings in the market were indicative of its inability to accurately price assets.

The second and most profound realization was a confirmation that this indeed was a systemic event and I had to act accordingly. My job now was to calmly plot a course of action to protect the wealth of my clients.

It was in these critical moments that I came to realize what I had been led to believe about the financial services industry was a big lie. I had thought that the management at Merrill Lynch valued financial advisors who were honor bound to fulfill their fiduciary responsibilities to their clients. The rawness of the situation left no place to hide for those who would shirk this responsibility. All during the summer and particularly the last three weeks before September 15, conversation around the lunch table had centered on an appropriate response to the strange markets. All of the pontification around the lunch table indicated that most of the FAs in the office, me included, were moving their personal assets to cash at an ever-increasing pace.

During the weeks that followed, I was disgusted to hear financial advisors on the phone urging clients to stay the course while holding cash in their personal accounts.

In the past, urging clients to stay invested meant that the financial advisor or broker was forgoing a commission that would have been earned on the transaction if the client sold their positions. This was no longer the case in the world of annuitized investments. Clients would have incurred no charges to sell C-share mutual funds that had been held over one year, nor would they have been charged a commission to exit the managed-money vehicles that were proprietary to Merrill Lynch. The only cost of selling annuitized assets would have been borne by the financial advisors as their trailing commissions on their clients' investments would have evaporated. This was an obvious and blatant undisclosed conflict of interest. The financial services industry's complete silence on this matter was an indictment of senior management's character, and the absence of a proactive response by a financial advisor was either an ethical lapse or a terminal case of denial.

In any case, the industry's failure to design (by properly incentivizing the organizational chart) a culture focused on the client had come home to roost at the worst possible time. The failure to even recognize the conflict of interest, much less do something about it, for the first time revealed the true nature of a culture in which abuses have flourished and continue to flourish.

The topic of conversation around the office was not centered on how we were to help our clients in their time of need, but rather on the humiliation of becoming a bank broker. In the world of Merrill Lynch, UBS, Morgan Stanley, and Goldman Sachs, nothing was a greater insult than being labeled a bank broker. Bank brokers had no sales ability. They survived only as order-takers from deposit operations and were paid accordingly. The macabre (to Merrill Lynch advisors) joke in the office was speculation around who was going to be required to sacrifice an office wall for the installation of the drive-through teller station, and how the office lobby was going to be changed by the soon-to-be installed ATM. I was humiliated because I had no answer for my clients' questions while the more experienced advisors in the office were humiliated because they would now be categorized as bank brokers. Mike Bling was inconsolable. To someone who had actually been employed outside the financial services industry, it was a surreal experience.

This was a microcosm reflective of the difference in attitude and outlook on life that estranged me from some of my colleagues. I am not staking out the moral high ground here. My professional experience had taught me that long-term profitability demanded a certain attitude regarding the client, and the majority of the attitudes at Merrill Lynch were different than mine. The empirical evidence would indicate that their attitude was much more lucrative since they were much more successful monetarily. Long-term I believed my approach would have won out, but we will never know.

Considering my fiduciary duty to my clients to be paramount put me at a great disadvantage when it came time to count PCs before my practice matured. As financial advisors at Merrill Lynch, we held a unique position within the firm because unlike other enterprises our first duty was not to the stockholders of the company. I will never forget the words of Bill Mitchell, who possessed as much integrity as anyone at Merrill Lynch. After I made the comment that the client had to come first in all considerations, he said, "Yeah, but you have to figure out a way to make a living first."

Over the next ten days, I noticed a pall settling in over the office as the lighthearted atmosphere that had made coming to work fun and challenging disappeared. There was no joy in Mudville. September 19 brought a new program from the Federal Reserve Bank to ensure money market funds as banks refused to loan to each other and a massive simultaneous deleveraging gripped the banking system even tighter. I just thanked God that Tom, Emily, and I had moved ARF's money into U.S. Treasury debt two weeks earlier, or they would not have been covered under the program.

It was at this time that Treasury Secretary Paulson put forth a proposal supported by the White House, congressional Democrats, and Federal Reserve Chairman Bernanke to avert falling over the precipice into the abyss. Although not considered esoteric, the proposal promptly evoked outcries from House Republicans and the populace in general of a government takeover of our financial system. I viewed Chairman Bernanke and Secretary Paulson as the only credible voices in this cacophony of political posturing. Both political parties were apparently ignoring the ticking of the financial doomsday clock. It was affirmation of my notion that the Congress of the United States was unable to act in a nonpartisan fashion regardless of the circumstances. If these fools could not grasp the seriousness of this situation and act as patriots, then they were not worthy of confidence.

The totality of the crisis was pushing me to make a decision that was either foolish or insightful, but one that could not be delayed much longer. With all that was going on, one thought permeated my mind.

I found myself trying to justify putting my personal assets in cash while making no attempt to share the advice with my clients.

As the market threatened to take a nosedive, the implications of sharing the advice illustrate the conflict of interest that was ever-present in the minds of financial advisors throughout the financial services industry. If we construed the situation as being systemic, then the only appropriate investment was cash or U.S. Treasury debt. This would of course mean the evaporation of my income and forfeiting any chance I would have of earning a bonus for 2008. There would be income upon the reinvestment of the cash, but who knew when that would be and who knew if we would be operating under the same commission structure. There was also the risk of sticking my neck out like a hotshot only to have the whole mess blow over in the coming weeks.

In the end I made the decision based on the potential upside versus the potential downside. I thought about Connie Speaks, who had just lost her husband of fifty years and was counting on me to protect the hard-earned life savings he had left her. I thought about all the people I had tried so hard to convince of my trustworthiness who were now, even though they may not know it, counting on me to do the right thing. But most of all I thought about Coach Ford, who had taken a chance on a greenhorn financial advisor simply because he perceived him to be honest.

By September 23 I had come to the conclusion that I was not going to spend another weekend worrying about the coach's money. In lieu of the usual phone call, early that Friday morning I set out for Clemson to meet with him face to face.

Coach Ford and I were really in the latter stages of the feeling-out process. I knew that impressing upon Coach the gravity of the situation was not as simple as saying I recommend we go to cash. That just would not have worked. This was no time for mind games or subtlety. If any situation demanded candor, this was it. I walked into Coach's farmhouse and told him that the ride from Blueberg had been a long one because I was not looking forward to this conversation. He simply looked at me and said, "Well, just give it to me."

I told him that I appreciated everything he had done for me and that there was very little in this world I would not do for him, but that if he did not move his investments to cash he probably needed to get another financial advisor.

I saw my whole career at Merrill Lynch flash before my eyes. The heartbreak of losing his account would be magnified by the call that would surely come from Don Plaus and the embarrassment of having the other financial advisors learn I had lost the account.

I told Coach I had watched a lot of football in my life, just as he had watched the markets. I even ventured to speculate I had watched more football than he had watched the markets. Then I pointed out that if I were made the head coach of a football team, I would have no concept of how to organize a practice or formulate a game plan, all tasks with which he was intimately familiar.

Then I reviewed the issues we had discussed frequently over the past month and detailed why I thought each one indicated a systemic threat to the economy. I explained to him that I was not making a dime from this recommendation; on the contrary, it was going to cost me commission dollars. I then sat back and waited for his reaction.

In typical Danny Ford fashion, he paused in reflection and came up with a great idea. He suggested we call his former financial advisor in Arkansas so that I could explain to him how I had formed my opinion.

It does not take Coach Ford long to get anybody on the phone. In short order I was talking with Max Benton about what I saw crashing down on the financial markets. He told me that he could not disagree with a thing I had said or the conclusions I had reached. He did say that knowing Danny as he did I had better be right. He was just doing his part to make the situation as difficult as possible for me in case he might lure Coach's account back to Arkansas. As the FA who had lost the account, it was his job to needle me. I handed the phone back to Coach, and he and Max had a brief conversation. Coach then hung up the phone and looked at me and said, "Do what you gotta do."

As I drove down the long driveway from his house, the recent drought around Clemson was being broken by a seasonal thunderstorm. I called Lucy Stone to place the order. Because of the rain pounding against the windshield, she could hardly understand me over my speakerphone. With apprehension in her voice, she took the order. I heard the clacking of the keyboard, and then she said, "It's done."

The following Monday I moved through the list of my clients holding equities and high-yield bonds who had risk-averse profiles. There were some necessarily dramatic conversations when clients thought I was overreacting, which was perfectly understandable. At the end of the day, most of the clients heeded my advice.

Their assets were safe, and what little income I had was gone.

Eleven days after my meeting with Coach Ford, Jim Cramer went on the *Today Show* and recommended that everyone who had money in the market and who might need it in the next five years should sell and take the money out of the market. At least now I had company and was taken out of the "lunatic fringe" category and put into just the "lunatic" category with Cramer.

Personally, I think that for Cramer and for many others on the Street, the last straw was the AIG bailout. In Blueberg another term entered the lexicon:

"credit default swap," which was anything but new to the fellows on the Street. This was a $45 trillion market that seems to have escaped my attention. When I polled the experienced financial advisors in the office, it became apparent that this had escaped their attention as well.

As I learned about credit default swaps and the malfeasance AIG had demonstrated in selling these instruments, it became clear how losses could appear on a balance sheet almost out of thin air. Credit default swaps were individually negotiated contracts between parties who were betting on a corporation's ability to pay their bonds. For instance, if you held $10 million worth of General Electric bonds, you could buy insurance that these bonds would be paid. The insurance contract was called a credit default swap. The price of any credit default swap was an indication of the financial viability of the corporation whose debt was being insured.

There were two problems that developed in this market.

First, AIG was writing insurance policies they could not afford to honor in the event of a massive loss.

Secondly, as the market matured, bets began being accepted from people who had no dog in the fight. In other words, if you thought GE bonds were going bad, you could go to any number of outlets and bet that these bonds would go bad. Because heretofore there had been no claims to pay, the companies that sold these credit default swaps were making astronomical profits and were paying outrageous bonuses to their executives. Since there was essentially no regulation of the industry, no requirements had been placed on the sellers of credit default swaps to hold adequate reserves in the event they would have to pay claims. The assets on the books of the leading financial institutions (ones that were too big to fail) were insured by swaps, and they received AAA ratings in many cases based in part on the fact that these credit default swaps were in place.

The value of a bond is directly correlated to the creditworthiness of the company or government entity obligated to pay the dividends and principal at maturity. With worthless credit default swaps backing this debt, the AAA rating of the bonds skidded into junk bond status and their value dropped off a cliff. That is how AIG, an insurance company, became the linchpin to the U.S. economy and even the world economy. Although enormously expensive, the rescue of AIG was a method to prop up many balance sheets and kill a thousand birds with one stone. (While this is an oversimplification, it will serve as a rough explanation.)

Although I had seen swaps listed as holdings in mutual funds, I never stopped to understand exactly what that meant. During my investigation, I took several courses through the Merrill Lynch University Web site, and I learned to my horror that there were interest rate swaps, currency swaps, and even commodity swaps that had derivatives placed on top. In other words, these were bets on bets. It became clear to me what Warren Buffett had meant when he said that derivatives were financial weapons of mass destruction. I now understood why no one knew how to unwind any of this.

The month of October 2008 shocked the markets but not my clients, and for that I was extremely grateful. Being right in this circumstance is one of the greatest achievements in my life, and all the credit should go to the man upstairs because without this relationship I would have never had the courage to take action. Faith in Jesus will make you brave.

14. A New Deal

They got the money, hey.
You know they got away.
They headed down south and they're still running today,
Singin',
Go on take the money and run.

– Steve Miller

I had always thought that Hank Patton was a stand-up guy, and so I considered his feedback as an industry veteran to be of extreme value. One afternoon in early October he had just returned from a trip to Florida, where he had visited a very large account. I wanted to check in to see if while en route he had heard any scuttlebutt of importance about the merger. I also took the opportunity to ask him if there was a chance there would be financial advisors in the Blueberg office who would seek employment elsewhere. He looked me square in the eye and told me point-blank he was sure there would be defections.

I knew immediately that Hank Patton, after eighteen years, was leaving Merrill Lynch.

The next morning as Sam and I poured our first cups of coffee we walked back to his office, and after securing his pledge of confidentiality, I told him that Hank was leaving. This was explosive information, and naturally he wanted to know how I had come to that conclusion. I refused to elaborate but guaranteed my prediction. Sam wanted to know if he could tell his best friend Reggie Sparks, and I asked him to refrain, and to this day I believe he honored that request. The reason I told Sam was that I knew he would be involved in the negotiations as Hank would certainly try to leave with as many income-producing brokers as possible. Given Hank's fascination with military history, he was surely planning his own personal Operation Overlord and enjoying the metaphorical aspect of the operation with an intensity nurtured since childhood.

Hank's honest, laissez-faire style of management and his position in the community would be a powerful draw for producers tempted to make a move. As a financial advisor with no income to speak of, and now even less since my clients' holdings were predominately in cash, I would be excluded from these clandestine negotiations and all manner of subterfuge that would surely go along with Hank's exit. I told no one else besides Sam Reagan, but I began an evaluation of each office advisor and the likelihood of their exit to the competition.

Against this grayish landscape of restless natives and protected clients, I watched as that fateful October unfolded. The markets had shaken violently back and forth until the first week in October when they began their descent. The panic that should have ensued when Lehman Brothers declared bankruptcy was now in full swing.

As the regulators and politicians moved in to save the day, our free market economy that had brought this nation unparalleled wealth and international stature dissolved away. It was a very perplexing time for free market advocates who could see the disaster that government intervention would bring but who also understood the unbearable cost of no government intervention. When asked if I supported the government bailout, I had no good answer. I likened it to drilling Keynesian holes in the side of the ship in calm water and then asking if I was in favor of bailing (no pun intended) out the water in rough seas.[4] I can't help but wonder what Adam Smith's position would have been. A John Keynes/Adam Smith[5] guest appearance on CNBC's Squawk Box would be a riveting debate. I am sure Smith would have advocated us going ahead and taking our medicine now. The dose we will have to take in the future will assuredly be larger and might be too big to swallow.

---

[4] John Maynard Keynes was a twentieth-century British economist who advocated a mix of private sector autonomy and the central planning of the economy by government's use of fiscal policy to spur demand.

[5] Adam Smith authored of The Wealth of Nations, which advocated a laissez-faire role of government in the economy contrary to Keynesian thought.

As the news began to delineate the fact that we were in a place economically no one had ever been, the future began to look more and more obscure. The election was right around the corner, and uncertainty reigned over the markets, driving them lower. In this politically transitional moment, the largest financial institutions in the United States were effectively nationalized. The government had decided that certain institutions were too big to fail and was left with no other choice but to provide them funds in exchange for preferred stock. It was surely the end of an era and would have by anyone's measure qualified under my early August prediction that before the election something will happen that we cannot contemplate.

It was in the last week of October that Don Plaus made his monthly visit to our office. I needed an audience to discuss my income situation in light of the fact that in protecting clients my commissions had been sacrificed. I walked into Hank Patton's office where he and Don were waiting. I jokingly reminded Don of my statement at lunch, which he obviously remembered, and I explained why I had moved my clients to cash.

I expected to be congratulated and given every consideration due to the seriousness and dedication I had shown in upholding my fiduciary responsibility to the firm's clients.

Don's reaction shocked me. He said, "So what are you telling me? You didn't adhere to the Merrill Lynch RIC report?"

The RIC was the quarterly research report containing Merrill Lynch's market forecast, which had not recommended selling.

Immediately Don caught himself and said, "So you were relying on Dave Rosenberg alone, I guess."

Stunned, I politely replied that I was relying on Dave Rosenberg, Meredith Whitney, Nouriel Roubini, and a healthy dose of common sense.

He knew what was coming next. I explained to him that I needed more money until things returned to normal.

Again his reply shocked me. "We eat what we kill in this business, and you knew the implications of putting your clients in cash when you did it."

In other words, if you want to get paid, get your clients invested—regardless of the market conditions.

I could see Hank Patton becoming a little uncomfortable because he knew that I was going to say my piece at that point. As I've said before, I admired Don, and I respected Don, but I did not fear Don. Very directly, but very respectfully, I told Don that whatever my sources and however I drew my conclusions, they had been correct. I insisted that there was no way to properly evaluate investments in this climate because there was no way to determine what an investor was actually buying. I flatly stated that battling the negative headlines that were an almost daily assault on the firm's credibility and financial solvency was making it next to impossible to acquire new accounts.

Our conversation was evidently in territory unfamiliar to Don in his dealings with financial advisors. The disapproving look on his face was unmistakable. Even though Don and I had had frank discussions in the past, they had been over the phone and not in front of Hank, who during the entire meeting sat strangely quiet, nervously fidgeting with his hands.

The conversation advanced, and to clear my conscience I had to say one last thing. I told Don, in the most nonthreatening tone I could muster, that certain issues had developed through the course of this crisis that concerned me. Speaking in a tone that inferred he already knew, I continued to explain that in my opinion it was a violation of a financial advisor's fiduciary responsibility to be holding personal assets in cash and recommending risk-averse clients stay invested. This statement let Don know I really had no choice ethically but to do what I did.

Obviously irritated, he cut off further conversation. He knew that Merrill Lynch had an even bigger conflict of interest with the large amount of revenue-sharing money and accounting fees coming in from the mutual fund companies, and he wasn't about to let the conversation go in that direction. He indicated the decision about increasing my commission draw was up to Hank and that was it.

I stood up, we all shook hands, and I thanked them for everything they had done for me and my family. I could tell that the situation with Merrill Lynch had taken its toll on Don Plaus. It is probably a good thing for him he did not know what was to transpire over the next two months.

In private conversation after the meeting, I asked Hank what had been the source of Don's irritation and got another surprising response. Hank said that during the tech bubble of the late 1990s, inexperienced financial advisors had luckily picked some dot-com stocks and been successful, only to crash and burn when the bubble burst. He said Don thought I had just gotten lucky, and it annoyed him. I failed to draw a correlation between my call and picking dot-com stocks, but it did not matter—both irritated the boss. Realizing there was no upside in pressing Hank for anything at this point, I did not pursue a further explanation. I just wanted him to quickly approve the increase in my draw.

The one potential bright spot in the lives of the experienced income-producing financial advisors was the soon-to-be-announced retention bonus that would be due from Bank of America. The bonuses were an industry tradition, and these FAs were waiting with bated breath to learn the amount of their windfall.

But management was dragging its feet in announcing the bonus amount. Primarily, management perceived that financial advisors would not leave the firm until they knew what the bonus would be and how it was to be paid. The other consideration was political. Given the fact that the bank had taken government money, a headline in the *Wall Street Journal* hailing the large bonuses being offered to Bank of America's wealthy financial advisors would have gone over like a lead balloon. Sam Reagan made the comment during this time of speculation that if the public knew the amount of bonuses they were going to receive, there would be hearings on Capitol Hill. Speculation was rampant, and all of the financial advisors were anxious to hear what the offer was going to be from Bank of America. In the meantime, they were also entertaining offers from other firms should Bank of America's offer prove inadequate.

Hank Patton and Bill Mitchell had attended an event for million-dollar producers in Arizona, and everyone was waiting for their return to learn what the rumor mill was generating in the way of bonus figures. The news from Arizona was not good. Bob McCann, who had never been in favor of paying large bonuses, was candid concerning the political climate in which Bank of America now operated. Over the course of their careers, Mike Bling, Sam Reagan, and Reggie Sparks had yet to realize the windfall awarded to advisors willing to set up shop with a competitor, so their ears were to the ground listening intently for information.

Even though I was convinced that Hank and Mike had already made a decision, I was not prepared for that sunny Tuesday in November when I returned from lunch to find that Mike, Hank, and Elaine had walked to the fax machine, simultaneously sent their letters of resignation, gone to the receptionist's desk in the lobby, put their keys on the counter, and informed the receptionist they were leaving and would not be back. Walking back into the office from lunch, the receptionist excitedly gave me the blow-by-blow of what had just transpired. Their move caught me off guard since I had not expected their departure to precede the much-anticipated announcement concerning the bonus amount.

I went directly to Sam Reagan's office and walked in the door. Looking up with a sheepish smile on his face, he said, "You nailed that one."

I asked him if he had been consulted about assuming the office manager's position. He was noncommittal. After deflecting more questions about his personal plans, we discussed who might be a suitable replacement for Hank. Over the last couple of weeks, I had noticed a kinship had developed between Reggie,

Sam, and Mike that had been noticeably absent prior to the merger. There were the lists quickly covered up in my presence and conversations cut short by my arrival. I knew the subterfuge was heavy and there was much, much more going on behind the scenes than met my eye. Things had just taken off before I anticipated. Now it was every man for himself because life had changed forever in the Blueberg office of Merrill Lynch, and there would be no going back.

Not being aware of the raiding laws that dictated how the protocol agreements were administered, I had to wonder why all the FAs who were leaving did not follow Mike and Hank out the door.

At home later that day, as I sat in my backyard working on a brick sidewalk project I had started what seemed like eons ago, I began to consider the motive for Mike and Hank to leave prior to the announcement of the bank's bonus offer. Since Mike and Hank had left Merrill Lynch for Morgan Stanley, it was obvious and undisputed that the move was not an effort to protect their clients or even to act in their clients' best interests.

Another thought that clouded my understanding of the move was why Hank would forfeit his enviable status within Merrill Lynch. I was surprised that Hank would leave the firm at a time when his eighteen years of service and all that he had accomplished would have earned him (and by extension his partner Mike Bling) ultimate consideration in an emergency situation like the one that was upon us now. One day Hank had all the seniority anyone would ever need, and the next day he was depending on Morgan Stanley to live up to an agreement written in a document. Morgan Stanley's past failures in this department surely did not escape General Patton's attention. The nature of what happened indicated to me that, in Hank's mind, Mike Bling was able to mitigate this aspect of the deal to get his big payday before the industry changed. It had also probably been an inside connection afforded by Hank's eighteen years that had allowed Hank, prior to the bank's announcement, to learn the amount of the bonus and to determine that it was not sufficient.

Once I realized this, the words of my grandfather Fletcher Blackwell, an old farmer with Mount Everest integrity, echoed in my ears: "Son, if you want to find out why someone's doing something you don't understand, follow the money."

In a lightning flash, I comprehended that the money was driving every decision that was being made by these FAs. (I won't call it greed because I am trying to be nice.) They would have gone to AIG if the bonus money had been there. Their only consideration concerning their clients was how many they could talk into moving. The very next second after that moment of clarity came another moment of clarity: Reggie Sparks, Harley Johnson, Sam Reagan, and Ted Tiller were going to be the next ones out the door.

A year or so before all of this turmoil, back when I was getting ready to graduate from the POA program, there had been percolating in the office a major alteration to the FA landscape. Being best friends, Reggie Sparks and Sam Reagan wanted to work together and were thus trying to form a team. Reggie was concerned that when Harley Johnson retired, Reggie would be unable to retain Harley's elderly client base, which in my mind was ridiculous. Reggie was exceptionally bright, well liked, and extremely competent. Reggie saw a remedy to this dilemma in a partnership with Sam and Ted, which to this day boggles my mind.

As a newcomer showing some potential, these guys were trying to include me in what would become known as the office "mega team." I was extremely flattered to be considered and was trying to figure ways that I might fit in, but after a while it became clear that there was an impasse that could not be negotiated away. This impasse was Ted Tiller. After everything Reggie had witnessed regarding the dysfunctional life and career of Ted Tiller, he was still willing to hop aboard for the ride. Nearing retirement, Harley Johnson really did not care and was amenable to just about any arrangement. I, on the other hand, was unwilling to be yoked with the worldliness embodied in the value system of Ted Tiller.

In discussing the situation with my wife Anita, we decided I would probably be better off to pass on this opportunity. The following morning I went in and told Sam that I wished him and Reggie the best of luck, but that I was going to step back. I told him that being so new in the business I did not know what I was doing or the implications of any decision I might be making, so therefore it would be better for me to just stay the course I was on. I did tell him that absent Ted Tiller, I would definitely reconsider my decision.

Now in the confluence of Merrill Lynch Blueberg and Morgan Stanley Blueberg, a defection by Sam Reagan would necessarily mean the others would have to follow. Since the first days of our relationship, Sam had repeated many times his prediction that Merrill Lynch would be purchased and that the subsequent bonus would make those in the right position rich. I knew he could never pass up this opportunity. I decided to place an envelope containing a note where only he could find it the next morning indicating that I was aware of what was about to happen. The more I thought about it, the more I wondered if I would have time the next morning. About ten thirty at night, I went back to the office and taped an envelope so that it would hang visibly over the edge of his desk in front of his center desk drawer. The envelope contained a note. It was unsigned and simply read, "I know."

The next morning he found the note and immediately knew its origin. I could tell he was annoyed as he insisted, "I don't care what you think you know; there have not been any decisions made."

At that time I was not aware that Morgan Stanley might be in legal jeopardy should Merrill Lynch be able to prove that any mass defection was coordinated. I did not argue with him, but he knew I knew and that was what mattered in the end.

On that Wednesday morning, there was no lack of tension as Don gathered the office staff in the conference room to debrief us. He started off by saying the office had received a body blow as a result of the previous day's events. He assured us he would move quickly to appoint a new manager and that the enormous book distribution would be carried out strictly according to company policy. He emphasized how lucrative this opportunity was for everyone in the office, and he urged us to pursue these clients with vigor but with respect for the rules of engagement. He said that it was not appropriate to besmirch Hank and Mike, but rather we should draw a contrast between Morgan Stanley and Bank of America. One has to remember that at this point in time Bank of America had been designated as too big to fail while Morgan Stanley was in the process of raising capital and struggling to stay independent. Their future was much more in doubt than that of Merrill Lynch, or at least we thought so at the time.

Given Hank and Mike's penchant for military tactics and history, their Tuesday morning departure (as opposed to a traditional Friday afternoon exit) had to be part of a carefully planned operation. I suspected that every move was orchestrated, and I accepted nothing as coincidence. If other FAs in the office were soon following them to Morgan Stanley, the FAs remaining behind enemy lines could be instrumental in blunting the Merrill Lynch counterattack.

As the accounts were distributed, I knew that Reggie and Sam would face an ethical dilemma. Representing to Merrill Lynch management that they were enthusiastically pursuing the accounts assigned to them in the distribution, when in fact they intended to make a halfhearted effort, would have been deceitful. I suspected Hank and Mike's plan in the aftermath of their departure included the "mega team" running interference on their behalf. It was a most interesting time to see the true character of these people I had worked with for three years boil to the surface.

I wish Hank had approved the increase in my pay before he left the firm, but the bevy of accounts I inherited (which ironically included his personal account) would more than make up for his slight. Besides the increased income from my new accounts, I also reaped another very important benefit. It was a benefit that only came from being on a team or having participated in a book distribution of this magnitude.

Looking over the allocations and the different investments Hank and Mike had selected for their clients, it became evident that these guys were masters at generating income for the firm. Since the financial crisis had taken its toll on the markets, as of early November 2008, the investment performance I had earned on behalf of my clients was far superior to what these guys had been able to produce.

On the other side of the ledger, the results their book of accounts had produced for themselves and Merrill Lynch were extraordinary. Part of that was because I had gone to cash, and the other part of it was Mike and Hank had a well-honed method of increasing YTB. The first time I heard Mike Bling use the term YTB in my first days at Merrill Lynch it was just another acronym in a sea of acronyms. But the second or third time he used YTB I bit and asked him what it meant. Mike was a habitual smart aleck, so you had to be careful asking him anything, but in this instance he was only too proud to say, "Yield to broker. That's what it's all about—yield to broker."

Analyzing these accounts and the different investments that made up the portfolios was my first glimpse into the secrets of the skim.

15. Revelation

There ain't no change in the weather.
Ain't no changes in me.
And I ain't hidin' from nobody.
Nobody's hidin' from me.
That's the way it's supposed to be.

– J. J. Cale

Just as my grandfather would have predicted, over the next two months all of the financial advisors with a sufficiently large amount of assets under management, along with their support staff, left Merrill Lynch Blueberg for the greener fields of Morgan Stanley's new Blueberg office.

There was one exception.

Bill Mitchell and his mountain of accounts remained in the Herd. Both Bill and Lucy Stone had considered moving, but both came to the realization that the logistical challenge was just too great, and they knew there would be opportunities provided by the simultaneous abdication of so many financial advisors.

Not only would Bill inherit some juicy accounts, his political sway in office decisions and up the management chain of command multiplied overnight. He was the only legitimate candidate for office manager, and I lobbied hard for his appointment. Even though he lacked some credentials and the exams he had to pass would add an enormous workload, Bill accepted the challenge. For a normal human being this might have been a hill too steep to climb, but Bill is not human, he is machinery.

With the exodus of Hank Patton and Mike Bling, a new unfamiliar species appeared in our office, and this would be the most difficult challenge of all in this brave new world. In a fashion reminiscent of the army that rode in to assist Tom and Emily, the bevy of underlings working for Don Plaus in Charlotte descended on the Blueberg office to supervise the book distributions and to conduct espionage to determine who was leaving and who was staying. It made the FAs who were intent on leaving just that much more anxious to hit the door. The guys and gals Don sent in were bureaucrats with a completely different style of management than Hank's laid-back way of doing things. They were almost intolerable.

One day Randy Dennis, one of the alpha members of the Charlotte pack, found a sleeve of golf balls on my credenza. In the middle of this hectic chaos, he insisted that Lucy Stone and I stop what we were doing to watch him stack, or attempt to stack, three golf balls on top of each other. For fifteen minutes we watched as he repeatedly tried and failed to balance the balls, one on top of the other, all the while vowing it could be done. He finally determined that my desk was not level and moved the show to the conference room, assuring Lucy and me that once he had a level surface, a miracle would be forthcoming. Having so much time invested, Lucy and I in some twisted form of hilarity were now willing to wait until hell froze over to see if this goof was going to be able to pull it off. After another fifteen minutes, Randy determined that these balls did not have the right kind of dimples and therefore deemed them not stackable. I could tell during the last five minutes of the show he was looking for an out. When the dimple idea hit his brain, Randy announced that tomorrow he would return from Charlotte with a sleeve of stackable golf balls. We never said a word to Merrill Lynch's version of David Copperfield; we just glanced around the room looking for the candid camera before returning to our desks.

Unlike members of the Herd, these staffers from Charlotte were well represented with minorities and females. Stan O'Neal had been right about the inherent discrimination in the culture of the financial services industry, which was in no way exclusive to Merrill Lynch. But his sledgehammer approach to remedy what he perceived as a discrimination issue was bound to fail because he misdiagnosed the problem.

Especially in the South, the financial advisory business is lily-white. When I was at Merrill Lynch, talented minorities were prevented from being successful in the brokerage business because the ability to successfully *manage money* was not the distinguishing criterion for achievement. In this neck of the woods, few black guys could backslap their way to $15 million in client assets by schmoozing wealthy white clients. (I am sure the industry can find several exceptions to the rule. One exception was the basis for a movie, so I rest my case.)[6] The same was true to a lesser degree for females. In the corner of my capitalist heart I have a sneaking suspicion that once talented minorities are given the chance to show that they can earn more money for clients than untalented backslappers, the clients' prejudice will dissipate. But trying to solve the problem by making minorities compete on the good-old-boy backslapping playing field is asinine. If transparency were brought to the industry, the backslapping culture would be doomed, and a level playing field would be established. Transparency, not affirmative action, is the key to unlocking the door for the deserving of all social strata.

The next-to-last team to leave was Richard and Rudy. Since I had refused to either lament the departure of my good friends or pretend as though I was not excited about the opportunity to retain some of their accounts, I had rubbed the future Morgan Stanley employees the wrong way. I can't say that I did it on purpose, but I certainly didn't lose any sleep over it. I knew I was not going anywhere, and my loyalty was to Merrill Lynch and my family. I took every opportunity to express the obvious conclusion that the financial advisors who chose to go to Morgan Stanley were not doing so in the best interests of their clients. Often I stated that even though I understood the importance of collecting that bonus, from an ethical perspective, acting in the client's best interests should have been the overriding consideration of the defectors. My proclamations were like fingernails across a blackboard to the soon-to-be-departed, and their obvious irritation uncovered most of the traitors in our midst.

Before Richard and Rudy made their break, Richard felt it necessary to pay me one last visit to share his infinite wisdom and issue a warning to me. He predicted that in eighteen months I was going to want to collect my bonus. My treatment of him and Rudy in regards to their clients would have everything to do with whether or not I would be able to cash my chips in at Morgan Stanley. Richard outlined for me the terms of the agreement that brought him from Smith Barney to Merrill Lynch, complete with a list of the individuals Merrill Lynch had agreed not to hire from Smith Barney as a result of his blackball. I didn't know whether to believe it or not, but I was extremely flattered that he

---

[6] *Pursuit of Happyness*, Columbia Pictures Corporation, 2006, is the story of a black stockbroker at Dean Witter in San Francisco.

respected (or feared) my ability to retain the clients for which I was responsible. Mine was the only warning he issued before his departure, and I was honored.

Remembering a conversation I had with Richard about a year earlier helped me put this situation in context. I had asked Richard if he knew one of the local gentry and whether or not this person was generally known to have a gruff personality. Richard replied that he could see how this person might be rude to ordinary people, but to him he was always very friendly.

After he had dispensed his parting advice, I just smiled at him and said, "Richard, you do what you gotta do, and I'll do what I gotta do."

This obviously was not the answer or the reaction he wanted or anticipated. As he got up to leave my office, he looked back one last time and said, "I'm just telling you."

My reply was, "Whatever, Richard."

And with that he was gone.

While the Bling/Patton team and the mega team were proficient in the secrets of the skim, the Rutledge/Mantooth organization was something to behold. As their client list was circulated around the conference table and the accounts divvied up, I realized why Richard had paid me that last visit. The list showed several pieces of information about each account, including the amount of assets and the amount of income earned annually by Merrill Lynch. There was one account in that list that had $445,000 in assets and during the previous twelve months had paid about $45,000 to Merrill Lynch.

There could have been several explanations for these numbers, including the possibility that the client may have withdrawn a substantial amount of funds, but nonetheless, those numbers, and similar figures from other accounts, got everyone's attention. Everybody in the office knew about the aggressive campaigns that Rudy and Richard had conducted marketing structured products, but we had no idea they were generating this kind of income. It really did defy belief.

All the FAs participating in the book distribution around the table openly wondered how Merrill Lynch's compliance department would have ever been party to this type of abuse, but we all knew it had because Richard and Rudy were notoriously omnipresent on that radar screen. It was also obvious that Hank Patton had been aware of what was being done as well.

After the departure of the mega team, a new FA, Flip Hebert (pronounced "ay-bear"), was brought in to partake of the bounty. This move by management was unexpected, but it should not have been. Flip had been in the Columbia office, where he had formed a pseudo-team with Carolyn McIntire, a twenty-five-year veteran of the firm, who sported a very nice book of accounts. Why Flip was being sent to Blueberg was not immediately clear, but no one begrudged him gorging at the trough because it had become so deep so quickly.

Flip was about thirty-five years old, of slight build, and recently divorced from a woman who still lived in Pleasantburg with their two sons. It was apparent from the get-go that Flip and Carolyn were he-in' and she-in', as they say down in Folksy. They made an interesting couple as Carolyn was pushing fifty. There was something more than his bow tie that made Flip different, but I couldn't quite put my finger on it. When I asked him what he was doing for the weekend and he readily admitted to being on his way to Columbia in order to paint Carolyn's toenails, I figured we wouldn't be hanging together too often. He had been with several firms over the course of his career, and he never spoke for an extended period of time without mentioning he had been the office manager at one stop. Flip was a CFP and knew his trade, but there was something weird about the whole picture.

Another interesting dynamic which we were not aware of at the time was Emily and Tom's imminent departure to join the others at Morgan Stanley. There had been some conjecture about whether or not they would leave because the bonuses they had earned upon their arrival at Merrill Lynch might be put in jeopardy by a premature defection.

One day shortly after Richard and Rudy had left, I was standing behind my desk and through the office window I had inherited from Bill Mitchell I noticed something amiss in the bullpen. I saw Tom and Emily, and something did not seem right about the scene. Just as I was thinking about walking out to investigate, Tom came into my office and told me he and Emily were leaving for Morgan Stanley. He shook my hand and told me how much he had enjoyed working with me, a gesture which I appreciated greatly. He then gave me some advice and told me that my mouth had always been my worst enemy.

I knew what he was saying. There would be little or no opportunity for me at Morgan Stanley, which suited me just fine, and I think Tom knew that. His advice was not vindictive or meant to be hurtful; he just knew that I would be inheriting some of his accounts and that being from Folksy our competitive paths would surely cross. The tenor of the conversation was completely different than the one Richard and I had had not so long ago.

When Emily had been attacked by the financial advisors at Smith Barney upon her resignation, Tom had seen how ugly these struggles could become. I assured Tom that there would be none of that from me. We parted as friends, and I count him so today. In reviewing his accounts, he had indeed understood his fiduciary responsibility to his clients, and I was relieved. In pursuit of Tom's clients, I tried to emphasize the differences in our approach. He was an old stock trader and stock picker while I was more of a portfolio constructor. The clients were left to make their choice, and most of them chose, understandably, to move with Tom to Morgan Stanley. Tom Hawkins is the type of man the financial services industry could use more of. He simultaneously treated his clients fairly and made money for himself and the firm.

I had to laugh at the reaction Richard and Rudy would have to the comments sparked by a review of their book of accounts. Emily would surely relay, with some embellishment I'm sure, everyone's dismay at discovering what Richard and Rudy had been doing. It was sure to turn up the volume several notches in the pursuit of their clients. I anticipated that when the topic was brought up around the lunch table at Morgan Stanley, Richard and Rudy would, in some warped mental twist, assume the role of victims.

I made it a point to inform each client who was trying to make a decision about staying with Merrill Lynch or moving to Morgan Stanley how much their trusted financial advisors now at Morgan Stanley had been charging them in fees and commissions. Some were shocked, and I don't think some of them believed me. To my utter amazement, some of the worst cases of abuse immediately forwarded their accounts to Morgan Stanley.

In many of these situations, however, I was successful in holding the accounts for Merrill Lynch and myself. Compared to the other financial advisors in the office I was having much more success, and management had recognized me for it.

When Rudy and Richard left, Don Plaus came into my office, looked at me, and said, "You are a made man now." I really appreciated Don's words and resolved to exceed his expectations.

At the beginning of November 2008, I was managing just north of $18 million in assets, and by Christmastime I was responsible for $89 million. As the New Year arrived, this number began to dwindle drastically as the transfer documents arrived from Morgan Stanley, but I was still able to hang on to a substantial amount of assets.

The task of managing such a large influx of clients is really beyond description. Every day the remaining financial advisors at Merrill Lynch struggled to service these accounts in the toughest markets since the Great Depression. It wasn't long until I realized that this was part of the plan hatched by General Patton. I am sure that Mike Bling's sales pitch had included assurances that the inexperienced financial advisors left behind would not be able to adequately meet the needs of those clients who were deciding whether to stay or move.

The new Morganites were well aware our workload weighed heavily in their favor, and they took every opportunity to call Lucy requesting administrative help to gum up the works even more. It was just more of the same disregard for the well-being of their clients, who were intentionally and subversively left in flux during the most catastrophic systemic event in the financial markets in sixty years. Unbelievably, because management thought there might be a chance to get the defectors back, the knuckleheads in management let it continue.

In an attempt to counterpunch Patton, the brain trust sent the golf ball stacker extraordinaire, Randy Dennis, into the marketplace to find replacement advisors to fill the empty offices at Merrill Lynch Blueberg. In short order Wellington Stewart, Jack Haley, and Roger Kendrick were inserted in the vacant offices around me so that Herb Camp could keep his place in the back. Ted Tiller's office in the corner was left unoccupied as was Rudy and Richard's old domain. Presumably these were left as bait to lure big teams away from the competition because, to no one's surprise, Randy had been unable to deliver anyone of significance.

Jack Haley was about fifty-two years old but had been in the business only a short time. He was smart enough to come over from Smith Barney after Randy, in desperation, ponied up an extra-nice bonus. Jack told me he had turned down Randy until he came up with a fairly outrageous figure. Jack was a nice guy who had a very good working knowledge of annuities and mutual funds, but he was never going to tackle large accounts. He had a great work ethic and was by far Randy's best get during the entire process.

Wellington Stuart was a Morgan Stanley broker in Pleasantburg on his way out the door when Randy rescued him. Wells was twenty-eight years old and a woman magnet. Tall, handsome, and single, Wells was put into the POA program (or whatever it was called at the time) so Randy could pay him a salary. Wells was an extremely nice guy and everyone liked him, but he had some moments. There were a couple of days he showed up to work in what we thought were the same clothes he had worn the previous day. Frequently his shirt looked like it had been pulled through a keyhole. A tennis player of some renown, Wells was certainly playing the field, if you get my drift. One day he came into my office and asked the question, "Hal, if your client sold stock and received $18,256, and he sold 621 shares, what was his price per share?"

So much for the stimulating lunchtime debates.

Roger Kendrick was a different story. He and Flip had been friends before Merrill Lynch hired either of them. Flip had recruited Roger, not Randy—although Flip thought Randy was the bee's knees. Roger had been an office manager at UBS before spending a short time, and I mean a very short time, with Morgan Stanley in Pleasantburg. There was obviously something about the situation that remained unknown, but I did not care to be filled in. Emily had tried to spill some beans before she left, but we didn't get around to having the conversation before her departure.

Roger was big and tall and a nice guy who had obviously been paid handsomely to make the move from UBS in Blueberg to Morgan Stanley in Pleasantburg. The reason he and Bill Mitchell gave for his return to Blueberg was that because his family's residence did not change when he went to Morgan Stanley, he had a very long commute to Pleasantburg. He was a smart guy and very easy to like, but he spent most of the day trading his personal account when the office (Bill Mitchell in particular) desperately needed someone to step up and produce. Although I was positive about not having the full picture and complete context of why Roger was at Merrill Lynch in Blueberg, I liked him and thought he was a decent human being.

In many cases the accounts I inherited had been mismanaged and were not appropriately diversified, particularly given the current state of affairs. I worked to explain to clients why adjustments in their accounts were necessary and touted the financial security Merrill Lynch now enjoyed being part of the Bank of America family. The strategy was effective for me as I was able to establish relationships and credibility with my new clients. My conscience is completely clear with regard to what I said about my former associates and the claims I made about Merrill Lynch's new solvency.

16. The Pecan Brief

An' I don't mind 'em switchin' sides,
An' standin' up for things they believe in.
When they're runnin' down my country, man,
They're walkin' on the fightin' side of me.

—Merle Haggard

A
s the scramble to solidify client relationships ebbed and flowed, there were occasional scraps with the former advisors. One instance that sticks out in my mind is the Pecan Brief episode.

In soliciting an account inherited from the Patton/Bling team, I had occasion to call one of Hank's former fraternity brothers, Dr. Lankston Moss, who was now practicing medicine in North Carolina. It was a fairly substantial account and one of the few inherited from that team that was not a member of the Patton family.

I spoke to his wife and introduced myself as their new Merrill Lynch advisor, and she promptly explained that she and Dr. Moss were committed to Hank. Graciously I told her I understood and personally thought a lot of Hank. In the course of the conversation, I asked her if she knew how much she and Dr. Moss had paid in fees over the last twelve months. I knew she had no idea.

Throwing out that kind of bait I was sure to get a bite because naturally she wanted to know. I promised to send her an e-mail with the information. Since it was Christmastime, we had a friendly chat, in the course of which I made the comment that I understood her reluctance to move her account at this juncture because she was due a box of pecans from Hank and Mike.

A box of pecans as was the Patton/Bling traditional annual Christmas gift to their clients. I could hear her smiling over the phone as she acknowledged my tongue-in-cheek comment. I suggested we speak again after her gift had been delivered. Mrs. Moss thought that my comments were funny, and we had built a small measure of rapport.

True to my word, I sent her an e-mail delineating the shocking fee amounts along with the comment that I hoped she enjoyed her expensive box of pecans this Christmas. A couple of days later I called her back; she thought the e-mail was cute, but she and her husband remained committed to Hank, which was fine. Before we hung up, though, she thanked me for my information and assured me her pecans would not be so expensive next year.

Shortly after my conversation with Mrs. Moss, Bill Mitchell came into my office. He clearly was carrying a weight of some kind. "Hal," he said, "I just received a call from Hank, and he is really upset about the e-mail you sent to Dr. Moss. He considers the remark about his pecans to be over the line."

Bill was dead serious, but it was all I could do to maintain my composure. Inside I was hysterically laughing so hard it started to leak out, first from my nose, and I snorted, unable to keep a straight face any longer.

"Bill, I didn't do anything out of line, and I do not owe Hank an apology," I said. "If I owed him an apology, I would call him, but that is simply not the case."

I could see the angst in his face, and before he could say anything I said, "You need me to apologize, don't you?"

"Yes, Hal, if you could do that for me, it will help me more than you know. Besides, it will allow you to take the high road."

As far as I was concerned, there were no roads on this map, high or low. This was just a case of Hank reaching back from the grave to influence events in his old stomping grounds and gain a little revenge on me at the same time. There was one sure way to cut his attempt off at the knees, and that was to simply pick up the phone and apologize. Bill was ready to press for my cooperation, but there was no need. I could tell he was grateful I had come around so quickly.

I knew that he and Randy were having conversations with Hank about coming back. I also knew the chances of that happening were exactly zero. Their attitude irritated me almost as much as their refusal to let go of the pie-in-the-sky notion that the main defector might return to the fold. The phone call was no problem; I was unhappy because management felt more loyalty to the traitor than to the troops in the trenches.

I was actually looking forward to the call. At some point in the call Hank was going to feel like the kid in kindergarten who had his candy swiped by a first-grade bully and now the teacher was making the bully express his contrived, profound regret.

The call went like this:

"Hank, this is Hal Blackwell. I just wanted to call and apologize for sending that e-mail to Ms. Moss. I guess I just got carried away when I disparaged your pecans like that, and I just want you to know I'm sorry."

"Well, that's okay, Hal. I know you didn't mean any harm by it."

I hung up the phone with a friend, but I still found the whole episode hilarious.

I judged correctly about the whole episode backfiring on Hank, so he was not ready to give up quite yet. The next day upon entering the building Randy Dennis made a beeline to my office, still encumbered by his laptop strapped to his back and his heavy coat folded over his arm, to curtly inform me that he needed to see me in his office (Ted Tiller's former space) immediately. I got up and followed him back to the sparse surroundings he inhabited three or four times a week, expecting to hear the details of a client's accusation that I had stolen something.

In some type of ninja move, Randy produced from the bundle he was carrying a piece of paper, no doubt courtesy of Hank Patton, emboldened with my treacherous words to Dr. and Mrs. Moss.

It's really hard to take a guy seriously once you have watched him try to balance three golf balls on top of one another for thirty minutes. In Randy's case it was even harder because he was about twelve years younger than me and had no other work experience outside this breach from reality known as the financial services industry. He had no idea what my experience was.

He began a speech he obviously had rehearsed on his drive all the way from Charlotte.

Again, I started looking around for the candid camera stuck in a crack or hidden in one the plants Ted had abandoned. Randy had this mind-numbing habit of asking questions to which the only appropriate response was "yes."

"Hal, do you want to be a million-dollar producer?" Hmm, let me see, I think the right answer to that question would be…"Yes!"

His questions were of this variety, mixed with the occasional bewildering inquiry:

"Hal, what would happen to tomorrow if the sun didn't come up?"

I wanted badly to say, "We wouldn't have to worry about these damned pecans any longer," but I just looked at him with a blank face and waited on the rhetorical nature of the question to dawn on him so he would move on. This went on for about twenty minutes. The sermon was a litany of disconnected observations interspersed with arcane and "yes" questions until he had had his say.

The fact that I had already apologized was not going to rob him of this opportunity. He had rehearsed this talk, and by gum he was going to give it. As his performance came to an end, he asked if I had any questions and braced to defend himself.

After that performance all I could say was, "Yes sir, boss, I hear you loud and clear," which really ticked him off even though I said it with sincerity faked rather well.

He wanted to argue. Randy always wanted to argue, but I wasn't biting on this, no sir. He got up and shook my hand (for what reason I have no clue). That was another thing Randy loved to do—shake hands. I took this as my cue to leave and walk back to my office. Inside my head I could hear the voice of Rod Serling: "You've just crossed over into the Twilight Zone."

The encounter left Randy unfulfilled and unsatisfied. The result was not what he had been gunning for, so before returning to Charlotte at the end of the day he decided to make one more run at me. His reaction to our conversation earlier that morning confirmed my suspicions: in a useless attempt to win him back to Merrill Lynch, Randy was trying to get his nose up Hank's posterior. Too blind to judge his efforts as hopeless, Randy was fast wearing me down.

On this visit to my office he came with a different tack. This time he had apparently opted for his tried-and-true method to drive home his point: the football analogy. Since I was a football fan, he was confident he could convince me to conclude that my e-mail to Dr. Moss had been out of bounds. He just needed to apply the right imagery and metaphor to get his message through my thick skull.

Settling into the chair in front of my desk, he said, "Hal, who is your favorite football player?"

"Jan Stenerud." Nothing derails a good football analogy like a kicker.

"Who is that? Who does he play for?"

"Oh, he's retired. He used to be the placekicker for the Kansas City Chiefs, and he was born in Norway—"

Randy interrupted me. "No, no, no, pick someone who's playing in the NFL right now."

"Okay, what about John Kasay?"

"No, no, no, pick somebody besides a kicker."

"Well let me see…"

"What about Tom Brady? Do you like Tom Brady?"

"No, I don't really like him too well…"

"Well let's just take Jake Delhomme. He plays for the Panthers."

"No, I really don't like him. Let's use Drew Brees. I like Drew Brees."

"Okay, okay, whatever," said Randy. "Do you think Drew Brees draws up plays right before the game, or does he practice all the plays with the team before they go out on Monday Night Football? What do you think? Do they practice the plays first?"

"Yes, they practice the plays."

"That's right! In the same way, before you send out an e-mail you need to go over it with your teammates so we can all be in on the play. Agreed?"

This went on for thirty minutes until my mind was numbed to the point I felt the man in front of me had turned into a North Vietnamese guard and I was locked up in the Hanoi Hilton.

"Randy," I said, "I appreciate everything, but I have to pick up my daughter in five minutes."

He got up and in an automatic reflex reached across the desk and shook my hand. He promised we would continue our dialogue at the very first opportunity.

The next day I went into Bill's office and told him he had to do something about this guy. He shook his head knowingly and said he would take care of it. Not a word of explanation was necessary. Everybody in the office, with the possible exception of Flip, was avoiding this guy like the plague. I could not believe he was in management. Randy was from Connecticut, had been an FA for a short while in Washington DC, and was totally out of touch with reality. All those puzzle pieces fit together in only one fashion. I figured his daddy had a very large pile of dollars in an account throwing off some serious fees.

About three days later, Randy came to continue the dialogue. Apparently he had slipped through Bill Mitchell's net. Even though I did not want to engage, I was forced to play the ultimate card. I said, "Randy, if you are so displeased with the way I handle my business, maybe I should just head on over to Smith Barney."

I never had any more dialogue with Randy except for the one brief attempt at resurrection he made, thanks to Mike Bling.

In spite of the fact I had apologized to Hank, Mike Bling took the initiative to send Don Minor, the compliance officer in Charlotte, a copy of the by-now-famous pecan brief, with his commentary on how even though it may not be illegal, Hal's words were certainly unprofessional, yada, yada. When Don Minor read it to Don Plaus on a conference call scheduled to put the matter to bed, Plaus just chuckled (much to Randy's disappointment) and said, "Be careful, Hal, but don't worry about it—you're good on that." I was smiling because written plainly between the lines in bright red letters was the message that Dr. Moss was getting discounted pecans from here on out, and the Bling YTB was picking up the tab. Mission accomplished!

17. Brush with Death

I'm travelin' down the road and I'm flirtin' with disaster.
I've got the pedal to the floor and my life is running faster.
I'm outta money, outta hope. It looks like self-destruction.
Well how much more can we take with all of this corruption?

– Dave Hlubek, Danny Joe Brown, and Banner Thomas

My job at Merrill Lynch went from being completely focused on account acquisition one day, to the next day being entirely immersed in the drama that engulfed the Merrill Lynch Blueberg office. One minute I was on the phone with a new client wanting to know if she should buy Boeing or General Dynamics for her grandchildren's $200 Christmas gift, and the next minute I was on the phone with Derek Cannon talking about $800 million.

My pursuit of knowledge and understanding of the financial crisis had necessarily taken a backseat in those hectic days, but I was still committed to staying abreast of what transpired in Washington and on Wall Street. In many cases it was necessary to explain to clients and prospects why Merrill Lynch was in the headlines. It was true that Merrill Lynch, now ensconced in the ample bosom of Bank of America, was much less likely to go belly-up than Morgan Stanley. The financial advisors who left could not rightfully claim anything to the contrary. The last thing they wanted to admit to their clients was that collecting their bonus money was their sole reason for leaving Merrill Lynch.

On the last day of December 2008, however, all of these claims of financial superiority came into serious doubt. On that day, the last trading day to be endured in the dreadful year that was 2008, a discrepancy popped up on my computer screen that I could not ignore. I noticed that there was a 21-cent arbitrage on the Merrill Lynch stock that was to be traded in for approximately .85 shares of Bank of America's stock at the end of the day. In other words, if you purchased Merrill Lynch stock that morning and the merger was consummated, you could earn 21 cents for every share purchased, which on an annual basis would have been in the neighborhood of 300 percent. I watched as the day moved along, and the arbitrage stayed in effect.

At two o'clock in the afternoon, I went to see Bill Mitchell, who now occupied Hank Patton's old space, and Lucy Stone, who now occupied Elaine Massey's former desk, and told them that something was amiss with the merger. Bill thought I was hallucinating. Lucy Stone was interested when I pointed out the arbitrage and asked for some speculation.

There was clearly something wrong, which meant there was a chance all of our ballyhooing about being partners with Bank of America was somehow in jeopardy. It was just another example of being a financial advisor with no ability to see what levers were being pulled behind the curtain in New York. The market is so valuable because it never lies about situations like this. There was no denying the shares of Merrill Lynch were selling at a discount with two hours of trading left before the merger. Bill Mitchell dismissed my concerns by pointing out that the regulatory authorities would never let such a devastating event transpire in this environment. I noticed, however, he wasn't putting in his order for any shares.

Even we knew the failure to consummate this merger would mean financial Armageddon. I held my breath as the market closed and no news hit the wire. In this case, no news was great news.

As we later learned, Ken Lewis had created a holiday nightmare for Hank Paulson and Ben Bernanke by threatening to invoke the material adverse change (MAC) clause standard to all merger agreements and back out of the merger. The deal was truly on the rocks, and this arbitrage was the first indication that the marriage between Bank of America and Merrill Lynch was going to have significant ups and downs.

Bank of America employees were going to rightfully be disgruntled by the destruction of their share price due to the $15 billion loss that only became apparent to some of the due diligence officers in late December. Because of Merrill Lynch, Bank of America CEO Ken Lewis was forced to call and beg the Federal Reserve and the U.S. Treasury for help with the deal, or he was going to have to invoke the MAC clause. This humiliation was on top of the issues Lewis was going to be forced to deal with because the losses were not made public before the shareholder vote to approve the merger. These events poisoned the relationship between Lewis and Thain before the ship ever set sail.

In addition, the Thundering Herd at Merrill Lynch was humiliated because the reckless, irresponsible, and downright ignorant risk-taking activities of the investment banking side of the organization had left them hat-in-hand begging Bank of America to take them in. To understand the degree of shame involved, remember at Merrill Lynch being labeled a bank broker was fighting words. For many financial advisors, this was more degradation than could be endured.

The ones who did not leave the firm turned this sadness into a fierce determination to prove themselves to their new partners and earn back the firm's self-respect. It was a trying time for all involved and continues to be a struggle for both management teams.

The merger did go through, of course, but the organizational strains made certain management changes inevitable. On top of all the confusion surrounding the merger, John Thain's problems were compounded by CNBC's on-air editor Charlie Gasparino revealing that Thain had spent $1.2 million redecorating his office. After indicating to his management team that he would be the logical successor to Ken Lewis, John Thain was toast. Greg Fleming, who had so brilliantly engineered the merger in the wee hours of that September weekend, had also bid the firm farewell. Bob McCann, who had so courageously advocated for the Thundering Herd when it counted most, was gone now too. Dan Sontag, the even-tempered leader who had risen through the ranks of brokers to lead the Herd after Bob McCann stepped down, was forced out almost immediately after he assumed the job.

The culture that had so many flaws was now sailing into a storm of fear and apprehension.

One of the few winners of this management debacle was Don Plaus, who was promoted out of the Charlotte office to run one of the four divisions of Merrill Lynch's wealth management operation. Despite his temporary defection to Morgan Stanley some five years earlier, Don had achieved heights that not even he expected. While I was glad to have a familiar face so far up the chain of command, it did bother me on a very deep level that Don had overseen some of the worst abuses in the Blueberg office. He had also been the one to discount and disregard my dedication to our fiduciary responsibilities regarding the sale of annuitized assets in the throes of the crisis. All in all, however, I was encouraged by my situation and was able to somehow rationalize Don's promotion as being good for me.

18. Up on the Hill

Well the night that was high, we got into town
Was the night that the rain, it froze on the ground.
Down the street I heard such a sorrowful tune
Comin' from the place they call the Spanish Moon.

– Lowell George

January 26, 2009, brought another Monday morning and my attempts to prioritize the commitments I had made to my new clients. At just about ten o'clock, my phone rang. On the line was Brock Morgan. Brock asked me if I could be in Washington the following morning at eight to accompany a contingent from Ag Renewable Fuels as they visited with different legislators in an effort to secure a government loan guarantee for the $800 million needed for their project.

Only a few weeks earlier, Brock and Derek Cannon had called me after a meeting with one of the largest ethanol distributors in Alabama. The news was not as good as they had hoped. I like to think of myself as ARF's biggest cheerleader, so they called to check in with me. They wanted to know if the lending situation had changed any in the economy or at Bank of America, which it had not. Hearing this news, they requested a brilliant recommendation from their financial advisor as to how they might address their predicament.

Given the situation, there was only one logical course of action, and that was to revert to the Willie Sutton principle of finding money. My suggestion was that in this environment Ag Renewable Fuels should explore the possibility of obtaining some type of government loan guarantee. Considering the sequence of events over the last three months, that option seemed to be in vogue.

The project that Ag Renewable Fuels was promoting was at the center of what the incoming Obama administration had outlined as top priorities. If the newly elected meant what they said, a renewable energy source and a step toward energy independence should receive a warm welcome in Washington. This phone call was proof that Brock Morgan had mobilized the considerable political clout the agricultural community had spent decades building, and things were moving swiftly.

The prospect of participating in this effort was exciting and an opportunity to step into an arena I had only read about. I told Brock I would absolutely meet him in Washington DC the following morning. I took the address of where the group was meeting to plan the itinerary before heading out to the Capitol Building.

I told Randy I was going to Washington with one of my clients and that I would be back on Thursday. Being engrossed in something on his laptop, he asked no questions but only muttered, "Okay."

In retrospect, I don't think he had any idea that over the next two days a greenhorn financial advisor would be sitting in meetings with some of the most powerful legislators in Congress. He may not have even heard what I said.

Booking a flight from Charlotte to Washington on such short notice can be a little expensive, so I decided to go by way of Baltimore and ride the train into DC (after all, that running back from UCLA, Joe Biden, rode the train all the time). Getting off the train in Union Station, I took a short cab ride to the hotel where Brock and the rest of the contingent were staying. Entering the lobby, I saw Brock and was able to briefly say hello before heading off to bed.

The next morning things started happening fast and furious. A winter storm had dropped a couple of inches of snow on the ground, and the flakes continued to fall as we made our way to the little breakfast nook three blocks from the Capitol to plan our day.

At breakfast we agreed on a place to reconvene during the lunch hour, and I was asked to join the group that was to spend the day talking with legislators including Sen. Lindsey Graham, Rep. Bob Inglis, and Rep. John Spratt, all from South Carolina; Rep. Allen Boyd from Florida; and staffers from the legislative delegations of other states that were to be home to the plants proposed by Ag

Renewable Fuels. The purpose of our visit was to have language changed in the stimulus package currently being debated in Congress. ARF had several key facets of their plan that separated it from the pack. As the stimulus package debate gathered steam, the buzzword on Capitol Hill that attracted the most attention was "shovel-ready." Derek Cannon had done an excellent job of obtaining the permits and all other aspects of site preparation, minus a few small details, which made the ARF project ready to start throwing dirt around immediately. These guys were prepared to create sixty-five hundred jobs within forty-five days. In the dark days of January 2009, these numbers were attention-getters.

The specific issue was line 9001 and line 9002 (at that time) in the stimulus bill that excluded from participating in the federal loan guarantee program renewable energy projects that did not employ advanced technology. ARF was not lobbying for a grant, just an opportunity to apply for a loan.

The bill had been worded to purposely preclude corn ethanol from consideration because of some misconceptions that had been publicized insisting that using corn for fuel was a strain on the world's food supply. The ARF group had ample evidence to refute this claim.

Another reason behind the exclusion of corn ethanol was to create an incentive for the renewable fuels industry to pursue cellulosic ethanol technologies. In layman's terms, the legislation was designed to spur research into making fuel from plants that did not have any dietary properties, like switch grass, algae, palm oil, jatropha, and, most importantly for the southeastern U.S. ethanol industry, pine and other tree cellulose.

The problem with this line of thinking was that *future* technology was not going to create jobs or promote energy independence *today*. The ARF plan offered an economically viable solution to many current issues and concerns. Additionally, the ARF projects intended to create an infrastructure that would facilitate cellulosic fuel research and the development of a supply chain for the technology as it came on line.

The good news was that Midwestern corn farmers were supporting ARF; the bad news was that the constituents of Rep. Henry Waxman of Beverly Hills, California, were not going to be swayed. ARF patrons were a constituency of Blue Dog Democrats (from the South mainly) and some southern Republicans powerlessly stuck in the minority party. The Blue Dog enthusiasm was heartening, but one could see the fault lines forming within the Democratic Party as the bill matured. Even as the grandstands from the inauguration still stood along Pennsylvania Avenue, the hard-core liberals and the Blue Dogs were staking out different positions.

Primarily because ARF was so late to the game, the lobbyist hired by ARF was pessimistic regarding the stimulus package. The legislation was being rushed through Congress at a record pace, and a detail such as the change ARF was requesting was just the type of sludge lawmakers were trying desperately to keep out of the bill.

From my perspective, I was receiving an education and the experience of a lifetime. Racing from one meeting in the House office building to a meeting in the Department of Agriculture and back to the Senate office building really had this ol' country boy from Folksy straining to take in all that was happening. It was an experience that made me not only a better financial advisor but a better citizen as well.

I'll also have to say that my faith in government was somewhat rekindled very briefly by the quality of the people on the staffs of our legislators. On their way to the lobbying profession, these products of America's most prestigious universities were keenly aware of the debates related to the renewable fuels issues and were anxious to hear what Derek had to say since he had valid, organized data that they could use. Between twenty-five and thirty-five years of age, these staffers asked insightful questions and demonstrated a phenomenal ability to focus on the crux of many of these issues with very little explanation.

The staffers would then confer with their legislator to formulate a policy—hopefully using the data Derek had prepared. I came away with the realization that twenty-five-to-thirty-five-year-olds pretty much ran our government.

I was also very impressed with Brock Morgan, Derek Cannon, and the other farmers on the board of directors of ARF who had come to Washington. These guys were experienced politicians. I had never thought of farmers as being politicians by necessity, but I quickly realized these guys knew their way around Washington much better than the institutional banking environment.

As the president of the United States Soybean Association, Brock Morgan had traveled the world, and he had run for statewide office, losing a close election. These farmers knew their representatives and senators along with many of the staffers we met with. I was impressed that on such short notice this group was able to arrange meetings with many of the actual legislators.

Sitting in strategy sessions with these good ol' boy professionals was enlightening and edifying at the same time. They took care to make sure what they said was absolutely true and accurate to the best of their knowledge. If there were facts that worked against them (as there surely were with a barrel of oil selling at around $35, down from $140), their plan was to agree but reinforce their contention that their business plan would work in the future by using hard data to define trends.

These guys clearly understood their credibility was the currency that paid their way into the halls of influence. Not one of them was willing to sacrifice or compromise their integrity for success with this project. They were keenly aware that if they maintained the validity of their word, this was not the last time they would be pressing the flesh in this neck of the woods. It was refreshing to see men who valued their integrity far more than any ethanol project. These were the type people I wanted to associate with and model my career after.

At the Department of Agriculture we met with the director of rural development, who had an office on the third floor of the DOA office building. When we got to the third floor and turned right off the elevator, I looked down a hallway that looked like it ran into infinity. I could not see the end of it. That hallway was longer than Main Street in Folksy. William Smith's office was halfway down on the left. Our meeting with him was significant because he was familiar with the type of loan programs of interest to ARF. Since Smith had been involved in several large transactions, he provided me more pertinent information regarding my responsibilities in the deal than anyone else we met with in Washington. The key tidbit of information he shared was that Bank of America had been very active in facilitating government-backed loans.

When I returned to Blueberg, I sat down and wrote a detailed account of my activities in Washington. I forwarded this e-mail to my superiors all the way up to Don Plaus who, as I have already mentioned, now occupied a place in the stratosphere of Merrill Lynch as a divisional director. The summation of the e-mail was that we had tried but we probably were not going to be successful regarding our efforts on the stimulus package. However, next up for debate in March would be the energy bill, by which time ARF would have had time to marshal its forces and make a more organized and effective push to have the needed language incorporated into the legislation.

At the end of February 2009, I again returned to Washington with Brock and Derek along with a couple of other board members. On this trip we were focused on making contacts within the new administration. Any faith that may have been rekindled in government by my experience in January quickly dissolved as we tried to maneuver through the bureaucracy of an administration that was largely unmanned. Despite the fact that President Obama had been in office for two months, there were alarmingly few positions that had been filled or were ready to be filled. It was a little unnerving, particularly the vacancies in the Treasury Department, where leadership was precariously thin.

The rationale for seeking government assistance on the ARF project was very simply that the shadow banking system and the securitization market no longer existed. To understand the significance of this and to provide an understanding of just how radically things had changed over the preceding six months, a brief explanation of these markets is appropriate here. It is also a story that reveals the moral turpitude that soaks the culture of our financial institutions.

In the United States prior to 1970, prospective homebuyers in various geographical locations around the country would be offered different mortgage interest rates. The lack of uniformity and inconsistency in the market tended to make for inefficiencies that could easily be addressed by the formation of a secondary market. There were many advantages to having uniformity in the mortgage market, but the primary consideration was the increased liquidity. The ability of the mortgage originator to be able to sell the mortgage instead of keeping it on the books and having to hold the commensurate reserves would make more money available for mortgage loans. This so-called secondary market would make it much easier for people to buy houses. To that end, in 1970 the Congress passed a law creating the Government National Mortgage Association, more commonly known as Gennie Mae.

If a mortgage loan met certain criteria (such as the borrower having been employed for five years, having a 20 percent down payment, a high percentage of income unobligated to regular monthly bills, and a good credit rating), the lending institution could sell the mortgage after it had been originated, for a profit, to Gennie Mae. This plan had the desired effect, and home ownership in the United States began to increase dramatically.

Shortly after the formation of Gennie Mae, two new entities were formed called Fannie Mae and Freddie Mac, which were referred to as quasi-governmental institutions, whatever that meant (although we would find out in the summer of 2008). The lending standards for these agencies were less stringent than Gennie Mae.

In 1985, a young computer company called Sperry had sold and financed a large number of computer systems to large U.S. corporations with AAA credit ratings. In order to provide Sperry with the needed funds to expand, some enterprising financier had the innovative idea to package this debt and sell it on Wall Street at a slight discount. These debt instruments inherited the AAA credit ratings of these large, financially sound U.S. corporations, which would be responsible for making the monthly payments on the debt.

Fast-forward to the spring of 2006, and we can see how an idea that was originally good, and good for business, can become twisted in the hands of greedy Wall Street peddlers.

Instruments like the ones sold by Sperry had morphed into a bonanza of structured debt products. There were debt instruments that contained credit default swaps, car loans, credit card debt, residential mortgage debt, commercial mortgage debt, and derivatives of all the above with different dates of maturity. The investment bankers would take whatever debt combination was the flavor of the week and send the prospectus to Standard & Poor's, Moody's, or Fitch (who, by the way, were receiving astronomical fees from the bankers) to rate this debt. How could anyone be surprised that to keep the fees coming, these rating agencies slapped AAA ratings on complete garbage all the while denying they had any conflict of interest? This will go down as the biggest confidence game in history.

The investment bankers then went into the securitized debt market and sold these pieces of junk at top dollar all over the world. Just think about the sums of money these guys were raking in. They had a box of paper for which they had paid the originator of the loan probably 1 or 2 percent at the most, the rating agencies a fee, and the principle amount of the note, most of which was purchased with borrowed money. Then these titans of finance collected the present value of the stream of income represented in the high-interest-rate debt instruments. Never mind that the chance of the debt being repaid on time to maturity was next to zero.

Once the instrument was sold, the investment bankers no longer had a dog in the fight. At that point they no longer cared whether the debt was paid or not because they had been paid handsomely. This was a moneymaking scheme on a scale that is just too large for people from Folksy like me to comprehend.

The problem for the investment bankers became how to find enough of this worthless debt to fill these instruments they were selling like hotcakes all over the globe. It was this greed and total disregard for the well-being of our financial system that spurred Merrill Lynch to buy First Franklin and for Lehman Brothers to acquire several smaller producers of subprime mortgage debt. Wall Street could not get enough of it and could not package it fast enough.

In these go-go days of unbridled greed, lenders were not asking the question of whether or not the borrower could repay the loan. The question was, "If I make this loan, how soon can I sell it, and how much can I get for it?" The borrower's ability to repay was of absolutely no consideration. There was no incentive in the system for anyone to care because no one's compensation was tied to the quality of the debt. It was a recipe for disaster from day one. The collapse of this market was a foregone conclusion that no one—not the regulators, not the politicians, and most of all not the purchasers of this debt—could envision. Wall Street sold this pig in a poke all over the world, and my guess is that as the truth continues to come out, our global neighbors are not going to be too happy about it.

The party did not end until there was the inevitable glut on the market and some of the securitized debt did not sell immediately. In blind greed, the management of Wall Street firms playing this game decided to hoard this debt that was now selling at a discount so that when the market returned their firms could realize an even greater profit. When the market did not come back, they were left holding the bag, and it was full of their own you-know-what.

As is the case in most economic bubbles, one day demand for the product can't be met, and the next day you can't give it away. This is what happened in the securitized debt game, and when the market glut hit the secondary market, it promptly collapsed along with the so-called shadow banking system.

As ARF sought funds in the post-securitized-debt world of finance, the playing field had morphed overnight to a massive deleveraging (banks selling this junk debt so they could raise cash to pay off the loans they had taken out to buy the junk in the first place) of the balance sheets on Wall Street.

The Wall Street firms had to raise capital because the people who were supposed to be making the payments on this debt they had purchased were not making their monthly payments. Imagine that! These streams of monthly payments that were not being made just so happened to represent an astronomical percentage of assets these jokers claimed to have on their balance sheet. These hotshot Wall Street bankers had invented the incredible shrinking asset, collateralized debt obligations or CDOs, and then loaded down their own balance sheets with this dead weight. Before awarding these bankers the Bonehead of All Time Award, remember—they walked away with personal fortunes.

As of the writing of this book, this deleveraging process is still in motion. When ARF started their project, the secondary market for debt was flourishing as would be expected in the last stages of a bubble. In the summer of 2008, bankers were forced to start asking all those old questions once again. No longer was the prime consideration in lending dictated by the secondary market. Bankers now had to ask themselves, "Can this borrower pay the money back, and how much must I reserve in cash to satisfy the regulators if I make this loan?" This was an entirely different question than they had been asking for the previous five years.

The criteria ARF had been trying to satisfy at the inception of the project was entirely different. Compounding the issue, bankers were, and still are, desperate for cash and not too interested in funding an $800 million loan that would be parked on their balance sheet without a government guarantee.

The only solution to such a predicament was the involvement of the government to back a loan, effectively putting U.S. Treasury debt (which is considered cash, for all intents and purposes) on the financial institution's balance sheet. Philosophically, this was a crushing realization and a situation I never thought I would see in my lifetime. Be that as it may, we went to work and were trying desperately to accomplish the goals of the organization. Needless to say, it was tough sledding.

Merrill Lynch's merger with Bank of America offered another glimmer of hope that we might be able to fund the project in-house, or at least allow Bank of America to help with the government loan guarantee. During the spring of 2009, the snag in these plans was some legal technicality in the charter of Merrill Lynch and Bank of America that precluded Merrill Lynch from referring certain business to Bank of America, or so I was told. Based on the information that I had been given, Merrill Lynch, by statute, had to wait until July 1, 2009, to resubmit the ARF project back through Merrill Lynch and over to Bank of America. There was a liaison designated to handle the Southeast Merrill Lynch referrals of this type. His name was Scott Cooley.

Having explained this to Brock and Derek, I was in somewhat of a holding pattern, but not Derek Cannon. Always thinking and always very aware of what was happening in his industry, when the situation changed, Derek redirected his thinking.

He had formulated a new project within ARF that sought to take advantage of the current distressed ethanol plants that had come on the market which were geographically coherent with the original business plan. Even though the original business plan had focused on supply chain efficiencies that emphasized the production of the ethanol in the southeastern region of the United States, if plants could be purchased that were situated on certain rail lines, then these facilities could be meshed seamlessly into the original plan. The best part about the opportunity was that these plants could be purchased for $100 million as opposed to the cost of constructing a new plant, which was north of $200 million. Becoming intimately familiar with all of the ethanol production facilities that fit these criteria, Derek identified two—one in Indiana and one in Ohio—that seemed to fit the bill. As we approached the July 1 date, it was clear that these distressed assets needed to be part of our presentation to Bank of America.

On several occasions I had told Derek and Brock that I might not be the person within the bank to take them to the promised land. In the summer of 2009, they had watched me work for over a year and seemed to be satisfied with my performance although I was not too proud of it.

They seemed to have confidence in me, and they elected me to the board of directors of ARF.

While I was extremely flattered to have been elected, there were considerations within Merrill Lynch that had to be attended to. Upon learning the news of my election, I immediately called Sean Blevins, our compliance director in Columbia. He directed me to a Web site where I filled out a questionnaire and submitted it to the home office in New York for consideration. I told Brock that until I heard back from my compliance department, I would have to sit in the board meetings strictly as a financial advisor and would not be able to cast votes. I assured him that as soon as I had a verdict from Merrill Lynch, I would be in touch with the board to make them aware of my status.

It was a real boost to my confidence as a financial advisor to have one of my clients think so much of me, especially men I held in such high esteem. I started to believe this mumbo jumbo I had been preaching to myself about always acting in the client's best interests because it would pay off in the end. I became more determined than ever to do whatever was within my power as an employee of Merrill Lynch to secure funding for ARF.

Derek and Scott Cooley, my new liaison to Bank of America, had a discussion that gave Derek some direction. He began to construct a document to illustrate the proposal, and Scott started developing a plan to get all of these options in front of the appropriate people. While I worked domestically, Derek had Mosh working to explore international opportunities whether they were debt, equity, or some combination of the two. Mosh agreed with me that, for several reasons, the distressed properties looked the most financially viable. The only questions that remained were the condition of these plants, the inevitable strings attached, and the politics that would be involved in closing any deal.

An ethanol plant is nothing more than an enormous liquor still. These guys were planning on making white lightning on a scale that would awe the most ambitious moonshiner. Never having seen one of these facilities firsthand, I was invited that summer to accompany Brock, Derek, Roger Hart (a board member who farmed about seventy-five hundred acres in the low country of South Carolina), Ben Walenski (an engineer from Fagan, Inc., out of St. Paul, Minnesota), and Bert Davis (an engineer from the railroad who lived in St. Louis) on a trip to the Midwest. We first visited the Indiana location and then the Ohio facility to see what ARF might be buying.

We landed in Indianapolis bright and early and then drove for two hours through a cornfield. At the end of the road was a giant liquor still that smelled like the carpet in my college dorm room. After touring the facility, we drove for six hours through more cornfields, grabbed a bite to eat, went to bed, and were out at the Ohio facility at seven o'clock the next morning. I learned that farmers don't necessarily move fast, they just move steadily.

Since these facilities were owned by a company in bankruptcy, we were escorted around each facility by James Torbush, who represented Nuance Capital, a New Jersey company which in effect owned the plants during the bankruptcy transition. Although James was only about thirty-five years old, his firm had participated recently in the Chrysler bankruptcy and other large insolvencies. Cautious at first, James warmed up when he found out we were familiar with Hilton Head Island, South Carolina, which was his destination as soon as he could get out of that cornfield. Torbush was an old name on the island, and James's description of playing golf at Colleton River Plantation and staying at the cabins in Augusta while playing Augusta National gave him immediate credibility with me.

At each facility a skeleton crew worked to keep each plant spick-and-span and ready to be restarted upon the delivery of a trainload of corn. There were some issues that concerned the engineers, but overall the plants looked in great shape. To me both plants just looked clean, new, and well maintained. My job was to pump James for as much information as I could in between golf stories.

From what I could understand about what James was trying to accomplish and what ARF was trying to accomplish, it seemed there were some undeniable synergies, and the longer we talked, the deal made more and more sense from a lot of different perspectives.

After fine-tuning the information memoranda that would be used by the bankers to evaluate the distressed asset deal, we submitted our proposal to Bank of America.

Bank of America issued a one-line e-mail reply: "For projects within the ethanol industry, Bank of America has no interest."

I was shocked that this potentially large deal had been rejected out of hand without serious consideration.

I called Derek to deliver the bad news, but he turned the tables on me. It seems that ARF had finally struck pay dirt in their quest to be allowed to apply for a government loan guarantee. His question to me was direct: In order to submit this application, we have to have our financial institution commit to facilitating the loan. Can Merrill Lynch supply the necessary documents? Immediately, the post-traumatic stress syndrome associated with the escrow account fiasco roared from the recesses of my memory. Embarrassingly, my answer had to be, "I'll get back to you on that right away."

I picked up the phone and called Kyle Rice, who was the business manager in the new regime that governed the Blueberg office since Don Plaus had been booted up the ladder. Bill Edmonds was the ultimate manager, but Kyle Rice was the person I needed to speak with about this matter. The so-called liaison between Merrill Lynch and Bank of America was in my doghouse, and besides, a call to him would've been useless anyway.

I asked Kyle if we could facilitate a government loan guarantee for $200 million in respect to the distressed assets in Indiana and Ohio. Kyle's flippant answer, "Sure, we can do that," immediately exposed his lack of understanding related to this very important question. Again the escrow account fiasco flashed across my consciousness.

When I asked him how we would determine the interest rate on the loan, he finally grasped what I was asking. Theoretically, a loan guaranteed by the government would represent a risk equivalent (and therefore an interest rate equivalent) to U.S. Treasury debt. Once he recognized that the rate would have to be negotiated at some level so the bank could get paid for servicing the loan and use of its capital, he did an about-face.

19. Standing My Ground

You can stand me up at the gates of hell,
But I won't back down.
Gonna stand my ground.
Won't be turned around.
And I'll keep this world from draggin' me down.

– Tom Petty

Kyle Rice is a bureaucrat's bureaucrat, and true to form he promptly referred me to Scott Cooley, the liaison who had produced the one-line e-mail of rejection from Bank of America. Dutifully I called Scott and filled him in on what I needed. He told me that he did not know whom to contact regarding a government loan guarantee. I can't remember exactly what I told him, but it was along the lines of, "It's a $200 million deal—find out, in a hurry."

Two days later I received a call from Kyle (I think because Scott was afraid to make the call) informing me that Scott could not locate the person within Bank of America who dealt with government loan guarantees. At that point I told Kyle that in my opinion Merrill Lynch had continually failed our client Ag Renewable Fuels. In the strongest terms this side of profanity, I spoke plainly and communicated in no uncertain terms that I felt the account was not being taken seriously and that there were people within the firm a lot more qualified than I who had not taken the bull by the horns and done all that was necessary to bring solutions to our client.

As I hung up the phone, my mind instinctively began to ponder what I was going to say to Derek and Brock to break the bad news gently. Suddenly a wave of determination washed over me as I remembered the conversation in Washington DC with William Smith, who assured us that Bank of America had participated in government loan programs actively in the past. I was not ready to give up quite yet. If I had not made that trip to Washington, I would have thrown in the towel right then and there, but I had come too far—and besides, this was a $200 million deal.

Through the course of my career I had learned that, when in doubt, there was always a place I could go to receive an answer to my questions. I turned to my computer screen, pulled up Google, typed in "Bank of America government loan guarantee program" in the search box, and hit enter. Lo and behold, there appeared in the middle of the page the name of Parker Weil, managing director, co-head of the America's Energy & Power Group, Bank of America-Merrill Lynch.

I knew what it felt like to be at Sutter's Mill on January 24, 1848, because I had surely just struck gold.

I opened up my contact list for the firm and typed in Weil, and the e-mail address for Parker Weil stared me in the face. I wondered if those bureaucratic blockheads in Columbia and Charlotte had even tried to find this person. The link on Google was to the Renewable Energy Finance Forum, which had been held in New York one month earlier. Mr. Weil had been a presenter at the conference, and the Web site had his picture along with an extensive biography. The site indicated Mr. Weil was intimately familiar with government loan guarantee programs.

Organizational protocol suggested I contact Scott Cooley to arrange an introduction. Since hell had not yet frozen over, I decided to take matters into my own hands.

I sent Mr. Weil an e-mail briefly outlining the situation and asking for his help. Forty-five minutes later he sent me a reply message via his Blackberry indicating he would be very interested to speak with me about the ARF deal. I responded by asking if he would like to have the client participate in the call and requested a time convenient for him to be on the call. Within minutes he suggested Thursday at four o'clock in the afternoon.

I called Brock and Derek to tell them we were in business. I tried to explain who Parker Weil was and the opportunity this call might represent. This guy was a big deal. You don't get to be a managing director responsible for two continents worth of power and energy without some serious gravitas.

Thursday afternoon rolled around, and after lunch I tried to access one of the conference call numbers so that everyone could access the call center as is standard practice nowadays. I went back to ask Lucy Stone for our office's number. She didn't know but suggested that I call Kyle Rice to get the number. She explained that since the new regime had taken over in Columbia all the numbers had been changed, and she had not been provided new numbers. I called Columbia and stressed the importance of having a response by three thirty so that I could send Mr. Weil (I emphasized "Managing Director Parker Weil" in hopes of grabbing someone's attention) the number with thirty minutes to spare.

I waited on a response that never came. At three thirty I called Columbia. Kyle's support staff wanted me to submit a form explaining the nature of the call and who was going to participate. They kindly volunteered to e-mail me the form.

I hung up the phone, went to freeconferencecall.com, and got my free conference call number in about two minutes. It was three forty, and there was no time to write an explanation on some bureaucrat's meaningless form so that Kyle Rice could justify his existence by calling me back to ask some ridiculous question. I sent the freeconferencecall.com number to Brock, Derek, and Mr. Weil, all of whom dialed in precisely at four o'clock.

Derek had done an outstanding job in Washington explaining the greenfield projects to legislators. In Indiana and Ohio, he conducted the meetings to evaluate the distressed-asset ethanol production facilities very effectively. I had seen Derek perform on behalf of ARF in several different situations, and each time he seemed to get better.

After brief introductions, Derek started off the conversation by saying that ARF was applying for a government loan guarantee.

Mr. Weil stopped him and said, "Do you mean Section 1037?"

"That's correct," replied Derek.

Mr. Weil then uttered some of the sweetest words I've ever heard.

"I am very familiar with the section. We are currently working on several other applications for other clients applying under that same section of the code."

While extremely relieved, I could feel the heat rising in my buttocks. As I suspected, the Columbia bureaucrats and my so-called liaison were of absolutely no value to me or my client. As the call progressed, it was obvious that we were speaking with the person for whom I had been searching for nearly a year.

Derek went on to explain the particulars of the distressed-asset deal as Mr. Weil's interest increased. There was no way farmer Brock Morgan was going to be denied the opportunity to discuss his beloved greenfield projects, and Mr. Weil dutifully took in all the information. It was obvious from the beginning of the call, however, that the distressed-asset deal was much more intriguing to Parker Weil than the original plans to build new facilities in South Carolina, Georgia, Alabama, and Mississippi.

I could not help but be impressed by Mr. Weil's knowledge and professionalism. It reminded me a lot of Don Plaus's performance in front of Coach Ford that night in Pleasantburg. I knew Bank of America-Merrill Lynch had this kind of ability, and at last I was glad to be a part of the team. The team in Columbia I was not so sure about.

As I hung up the phone, I felt a tremendous relief. Finally, I had fulfilled my obligation to Ag Renewable Fuels. I still desperately wanted them to get funding and hoped that with Parker Weil's help they would find that pot of gold, but regardless of the outcome I had lived up to the promise I had made over one year ago to the board of directors in Jasper Hills, Alabama.

I walked out of my office and headed for the corner to give Bill Mitchell and Lucy Stone the news that now the monkey was off my back. They had watched over the course of a year as I had journeyed to Washington, braved the cornfields of the Midwest, and agonized over the apparent apathy of management, always pressing forward on behalf of the client. I felt pretty good about the whole situation, and if I made a pot full of money off of the deal all the better. In the course of working on this deal, I had seen and learned more than money could buy. I had met men of high integrity and seen them operate at the highest levels. A fat paycheck, earned fair and square, would top it off nicely.

20. Somewhere Down The Track

Harry got up, dressed all in black
Went down to the station, and he's never coming back.
They found his clothing scattered somewhere down the track,
And he won't be down on Wall Street in the morning.

– Don Henley, Danny Kortchmar, and Jai Winding

Since the beginning of the financial crisis of 2008, the vultures had been circling over the Thundering Herd at Merrill Lynch. The chief vulture in Blueberg was Dick Plum, the office manager at Smith Barney, who had suffered two defeats at the hands of our former leader, Hank Patton. Dick was now in hot pursuit of Bill Mitchell and me. One of the interesting developments in early 2009 was the merger of Morgan Stanley and Smith Barney (which had been a part of Citigroup). The official name of the new firm was Morgan Stanley Smith Barney, but at Merrill Lynch we just called it "Citi Morgue" for short.

Although currently in two different offices, the plans were to bring all of the old Blueberg warhorses together in new luxury suites on Main Street as soon as possible. This would put Richard back with the people he had black-balled from following him to Merrill Lynch and Emily back together with the people who had made a frontal assault on her personally, as well as her book of accounts, back in 2005.

As much as I competed with the folks who went to Morgan Stanley, at lunchtime I missed them. I even missed Ted Tiller and Mike Bling. The new group was not as feisty as the old barb slingers. There was no banter, no iron sharpening iron, and I found myself more and more becoming the office cynic simply out of boredom.

The steady stream of wholesalers was now a trickle due to the heavy hitters being at Morgan Stanley, and the lunch forum was replaced with Bill Mitchell's new Tuesday morning sales meetings. Hank Patton was the self-admitted Fred Flintstone of the office technology. You could not communicate with him via e-mail. He did not know how to open his inbox much less reply to an e-mail he received. When all other possible methods of correspondence had been eliminated and Elaine was not in the office, he typed with one finger. Yes, Hank had his shortcomings, but in three years Hank never held a sales meeting per se. Is it any wonder we all loved him?

The new Tuesday morning sales meetings started at eight thirty, which made it impossible for Herb Camp to consistently attend. He might show, he might not, and in the first six months of this new routine he was batting slightly better than .500 for being present for at least part of the meeting. I never recall him arriving on time. This despite the fact that every day he parked on the street because he was too lazy to walk to his office from the parking lot like everyone else.

His dedication to underperformance would have been hard enough to stomach, but since the split Herb had taken on a more sinister role: double agent. On several occasions in his steady stream of conversation, it slipped out that he was having regular conversations with his friends at Morgan Stanley. No reasonable human could have safely considered any information shared with Herb as not being shared with the competition. The existence of his admitted conversations meant that, intentionally or unintentionally, it was possible he was sharing information with the competition.

This galled me to no end. Having this specter looming over the office was unacceptable. In an attempt to mitigate the effects of Herb's treason, I started feeding him false information. Bill and I spoke about the situation several times, but according to management, there were just too many accounts and too few FAs to address the situation.

Roger and Flip were gone most of the time. No one really knew where Roger's out-of-office escapades took him. Jack Haley and Nick Neapolitan were there every Tuesday, on time. Wells attended regularly and as a part of his pledging activities was responsible for a five-minute info segment at the conclusion of each meeting. These were consistently a disaster, so much so I stopped giving him grief about it.

Flip had a good reason to be absent, however. Besides being in constant pursuit of Carolyn's toenails, the Flipper was developing a market niche and strategy that required travel. It seems that he had perfected a spiel to attorneys who catered to the gay and lesbian community. He had learned a neat little feature of the estate laws that provided certain advantages for same-sex couples through the use of a Crummy Trust, which was originally designed to permit tax-free gifts of cash to children.

Flip loved to come into my office and regale me with stories of the gay lifestyle he had witnessed or how he had been able to impress some gay lawyer with his extensive knowledge of grantor trusts.

Bank of America aggressively courts the gay market. Even though he was straight, Flip was trying to be the go-to guy on all matters homosexual. He seemed to be making headway. His travel demands related to his strategy of visiting Merrill Lynch offices located in gay hot spots and educating the advisors on how to approach this demographic (for half the PCs generated, of course). He had a mobile rainbow booth complete with the Bank of America gay & lesbian marketing brand and literature designed for conventions and conferences.

My fear was that word might leak out in Blueberg, the proverbial buckle on the Bible belt. I suspected that Bill Mitchell was well aware of this fact of life and made some arrangements before agreeing to take Flip in. I say this because much to everyone in the office's relief, Flip did not attend the first annual Gay Pride parade down Main Street in Blueberg.

In their undying devotion to mediocrity, all the other FAs were on cruise control, trying to avoid management's radar screen. Nick was trying to overcome a dismal retention rate on the accounts he had inherited from the defections. His lack of sales experience and Canadian roots were making it a tough go. He was an honest guy and was managing to hang in there despite some personal strife. The lack of warm bodies definitely worked in his favor as it did for Wells and Herb.

Flip and I were constantly vying for second place in office production behind the million-dollar man and office manager Bill Mitchell. Since the exit of Ted Tiller, the office now had a three-ring binder that kept a daily record of money earned for the firm per producer. Ted's lack of new production had moved him to ban the practice before my arrival.

I was a little surprised Roger Kendrick was not making a better showing. When Roger joined our office, Flip made it clear that since he and Roger had at one time been in management, they were going to guide Bill along until he got his sea legs. Flip never missed an opportunity to stop by my office to tell me that since he had been a manager he was interviewing a potential new hire, or since he had been a manager he had been asked to do this or that. The repetition of this manifestation of his little-man syndrome went on ad infinitum and got under most everyone's skin—in particular that of Lucy Stone, Jack Haley, and me.

At lunch one day, Flip was indulging in another one of his favorite topics of conversation—his work ethic—and it became just a little too much for me to take. When someone feels the regular need to tell me how much they are working, being from Folksy I just naturally assume they aren't working very much. When Flip was in the office, most of his time was spent just walking around telling everyone how late he had stayed in the office the night before or how late he planned on staying that night. I was hoping that someone would tell him that if he would go sit down and do his job, the hours really weren't that bad.

The atmosphere in the office was such a contrast to the good ole days. I began to reflect on the caustic nature of my attitude. Wells had been the recipient of some pretty sharp barbs. In one instance I felt the need to go apologize to him. I was losing my "attitude of gratitude" outlook on life. These people thrived on mediocrity while doing as little as possible, and it was wearing on me.

The crew that left for Morgan Stanley surely had their issues, but lack of drive and lack of gray matter was not among them. The apathy that permeated the office was offensive to me, and coupled with the incompetence from the support staff on the ARF deal, the whole situation was depressing.

In late July of 2009, the writing was on the wall. My only real chance to earn a decent living in this new environment was to partner with Bill Mitchell or change firms. Bill and I had talked about this, and I had even included him in a $2 million relationship I was in the process of engineering away from Smith Barney. (It was the first account of any size brought into the Blueberg office post merger.) This was a large account for Bill, and we ultimately were successful moving the account, but he was in no hurry to accommodate my ambition. None of the other opportunities in the Blueberg Merrill Lynch office were even a remote partnership possibility. I remembered the leverage that Reggie and Mike had ultimately been forced to apply to achieve their partnerships, and so I started laying the groundwork.

Every Saturday for the last year I had received a piece of mail from Dick Plum at Smith Barney. My wife was amused and somewhat amazed at how much paper Smith Barney had sent to me over the course of a year. Aside from Morgan Stanley (and I surely wasn't going down that road since the merger was not yet fully integrated), Smith Barney was the only other real option in Blueberg. Dick and I made plans to have breakfast at a top-secret rendezvous scheduled the following week.

Dick was a cordial gentleman and was very well met. A former fighter pilot, he appeared at the meeting neatly dressed in an expensive suit with his white hair closely cut. But surprisingly he was ten minutes late. I shook his hand, expecting an explanation for his late arrival, but none was forthcoming. This gave me an impression of arrogance I should have expected. Unlike the meeting with Scott Hotham so many years ago, Dick's attitude came off not as confident, but haughty.

In the first ten minutes of getting acquainted, it was obvious this guy wasn't in Hotham's league. We chatted for a while, and he told me what information he required in order to extend me an official letter containing the terms of the deal. I told him this was my first experience shopping my talents and potential book of accounts like this and I had no idea what I was doing. This is a strategy I had seen Coach Ford use on a couple of occasions. It was designed to give charlatans or incompetents just enough rope to hang themselves.

I could see Dick shift in his chair as he studied me and took in what I had just said. It was obvious that transparency made him uncomfortable, and I could tell he was in new territory. He referenced a client spreadsheet that was produced by the Merrill Lynch software. Once this spreadsheet was in hand, he would handle the rest. I promised to begin accumulating the information and send it to him. This was not a lie because I planned to negotiate an offer with him, but a greater comfort level would be required before I would hand over what he wanted to see. First, however, I was going to see how well he guided me. I wanted to see if he would make an attempt to take advantage of my openness. On two different occasions in the conversation I emphasized that I was placing my career in his hands and he was the man I was counting on to protect me.

Over the next week Dick and I spoke once or twice, and during the last call I asked for another meeting, to which he readily agreed. To my knowledge the only success Dick had had in procuring producers from other firms was a woman formerly with A.G. Edwards. From the scuttlebutt around town, she seemed to be a fairly heavy hitter who knew what she was doing. The other evaluations of Dick's shop indicated he needed more bodies pretty quickly.

At this second meeting, in an effort to avoid any surprises, I shared with Dick my criminal record.

In 1985, before I left Columbia, South Carolina, for the deep forest of western North Carolina to be a summer camp counselor, I closed my checking account. Unfortunately, two checks, one for $35 and one for $7.35, had not cleared. My roommates at the time didn't seem to think those letters from the bank to be all that important. Upon my return from being incommunicado, I immediately took care of the matter through an attorney who I thought had made arrangements to have my record expunged.

Twelve years later, when I was in the insurance business, I had been given $5 million binding authority for the Hartford Insurance Group, which meant I could sign documents issuing immediate coverage for that amount. Up until that time, I was the youngest person to have been given this authority in South Carolina. I also had power of attorney to sign Hartford performance bonds in the same amount. There were similar arrangements with Zurich Insurance, State Auto Insurance, and several other major insurance carriers.

These authorities granted to me led me to assume that I had no skeletons in my closet.

In 2005, when I came to Merrill Lynch and filled out my Form U4 (Uniform Application for Broker-Dealer Registration), I made the honest mistake of saying I had no criminal record. Because I had told him about the incident during the interviewing process but insisted the matter had been resolved, Hank Patton had come to my rescue. I was allowed to file another U4. (On the FINRA Web site, a list of all the brokers under their authority is available to the public, along with any "disclosures." Sure enough, one of the unspecified disclosures is "criminal," which lumps me in with embezzlers, drunk drivers, people arrested for drug possession, and all the other offenders who are now licensed to sell investments.)

I can't remember what I purchased twenty-five years ago that turned out to be so expensive. I hope the items were on sale.

I felt Dick needed to know this up front, so I told him.

His reaction surprised me. He seemed to think less of me as a person, which I thought was a poor way to assess the trustworthiness of a potential candidate.

Despite the judgmental vibe, he asked me for my spreadsheet. I told him that I been unable to rummage through the Merrill Lynch software and find a spreadsheet that did not include the account numbers of my clients. I asked Dick point-blank if according to the protocol advisors were allowed to take this information. He said that he felt sure it was permissible but that he would get back to me with a definite answer.

At that point alarm bells went off. I had placed my career in the hands of someone who was supposed to arrange advisor defections for a living, and he did not know this answer? (Managers at Smith Barney don't have clients—their singular focus is to manage the office.)

Immediately after the Blueberg mass exodus to Morgan Stanley, Randy Dennis had been investigating any possible violations of the protocol as a part of planning the Merrill Lynch counterattack. In one of his diatribes (before he was given the assignment to woo the advisors back into the fold), Randy had made the statement that one of the disenfranchised advisors had taken clients' account numbers in violation of the protocol agreement. This led me to the conclusion that either Dick Plum did not know what he was doing, or he had a hidden agenda. Either way, I was cutting this process off right away.

I was a little bit sad about this development. Smith Barney had the largest market share in Blueberg and the heaviest hitters in town. Several of the teams in that office might have offered me a lucrative opportunity at some point in the future.

The other interesting dynamic was the soon-to-be combining of the Morgan Stanley office with their new Smith Barney brethren. Even though Morgan Stanley had purchased Smith Barney from disgraced Citigroup, the politics in Blueberg would be the polar opposite of the national scene. The size of the egos in the Smith Barney office was commensurate with the size of their book of accounts and Blueberg market share.

The advisors at Smith Barney are well aware of Ted Tiller's issues, and will be ruling that roost when the day comes that the offices are combine as required by the merger. Richard and Emily are also in a predicament as the day when all the affected advisors prepare to hold hands and sing "Kumbaya" looms closer and closer. I would liked to warm myself by that campfire and to see those sparks fly. Being on the other side of the fence would have offered an interesting perspective as the old Merrill Lynch gang grappled for terra firma in the shifting sands of that merger.

On August 12, 2009, I was scheduled to be a presenter at the Southeastern Bio Fuels conference in Tifton, Georgia. The theme was "Finding Funding in a Challenging Market." Before leaving for Georgia, I stopped in to tell Bill that my conversations with Dick had taken on new meaning recently and that we could talk when I returned. Several times Bill and I had discussed Dick's efforts to recruit us, but this time it was important for him to understand the seriousness of what was going on. I told Bill because the idea of pulling something like the other advisors had done was not in my makeup.

Along the path that Lucy, Bill, and I had traveled over the last surreal months, I had made a commitment to Bill and to Merrill Lynch. Industry tradition notwithstanding, walking in one Friday afternoon with my resignation was not my style. In addition to letting Bill in on the discussions, I decided to let Merrill Lynch management in on it as well.

Into a file on my desktop I downloaded a copy of the spreadsheet Dick had referenced. I immediately opened the file and deleted the information a defecting broker would not be allowed to have. I knew such an action would set off the electronic spies lurking within my desktop computer, but most importantly I knew that Bill Mitchell knew that my computer skills were such that I was fully aware that I was being watched.

Upon my return from Georgia, I stopped by Bill's office to tell him that the Smith Barney issue was no longer an issue. I frankly told him about my doubts surrounding Dick Plum's strange lapse of memory concerning what information was permitted according to the protocol. I shared with him my speculation that there were really only two explanations. One was that he had an honest lapse of memory. The other was that he was trying to create some problems for me. I told him these antics had cooled my enthusiasm and that I had made a decision to stay with Merrill Lynch.

He told me that moving now would not have been a smart move because my deal at Smith Barney depended on my trailing twelve-month commissions, and waiting until January of 2010 would allow me to include the big boost in revenue as a result of the accounts I had inherited. My position was not about the timing issue; it had more to do with the people involved.

21. Before the Court

So there I was in Hollywood
Thinking I was doing good,
Talking on the telephone line.
They don't want me in the movies
And nobody sings my songs;
My mama says my baby's doing fine.

—Danny Flowers

Later that same day, Bill Mitchell told me that he needed to speak with me, not in his office (where Lucy could hear) but in the conference room. We walked down the hall to the conference room, and when the door was closed he said that he needed to ask me some questions on behalf of the legal team at Merrill Lynch. He was extremely uncomfortable, and I tried to put him at ease by signaling that he had my complete cooperation with whatever it was he had to do.

Immediately it was clear that Kyle Rice was aware of the spreadsheet I had downloaded.

I said fine, shoot.

Question: Are you planning to resign from Merrill Lynch?

Answer: No.

Question: Have you discussed plans to leave Merrill Lynch with any of your clients?

Answer: No.

Question: Have you provided Merrill Lynch information to persons outside the firm?

Answer: No.

Bill apologized for having to ask me these questions, but I could tell there was more. He then stated that Merrill Lynch wanted to scrub my personal computer that contained the information I had e-mailed to my home. I said no problem even though this did irk me. I wanted the Merrill Lynch espionage unit to know I had nothing to hide, so I went straight home to retrieve my personal computer. Looking at it would prove to the legal team that I had answered the three questions truthfully. I wanted them to see where I had erased the information not permitted by the protocol, and that I had neither forwarded it nor printed it.

Handing it over, I asked Bill if they wanted my password to facilitate looking at the machine. I also provided the password to my Internet-based e-mail account with Gmail in case they wanted to snoop around in there as well. I wanted them to know beyond a shadow of a doubt my words were true.

About a week later the laptop was returned, followed shortly thereafter by an e-mail note from Kyle Rice saying Merrill Lynch had found nothing of concern on my computer and thanking me for my help in the process. I sent an e-mail back saying I enjoyed being proven innocent.

This episode followed closely on the heels of the tête-à-tête I had with Kyle Rice about the service Ag Renewable Fuels had been receiving. Shortly after the exonerating e-mail, Kyle called me to ask some questions that really took me by surprise. He wanted to know all about my trip to Washington with ARF and my election to their board of directors. After discussing this with him for a short period, I offered to forward him all the documents I had relating to the matter.

He was concerned that ARF was expecting more from me than I could deliver. What a classic bureaucratic, cowardly response to our previous conversation! I could hardly believe my ears. I suggested we write ARF a letter and outline specifically what he felt needed to be communicated about my role as their financial advisor. He thought that was a good idea, but he wanted to think about it first. In other words, this really wasn't about making sure the client had a clear picture of what was going on—this was an internal matter that had absolutely nothing to do with the client.

Kyle's next remarks confirmed the conclusion I had drawn from his luke-warm response to my letter idea. He said that management had discovered a LinkedIn account with my information. This was prohibited by Merrill Lynch, and he asked if I would remove it. When I logged in to erase the information, I noticed the site had garnered two hits: mine and whoever at Merrill Lynch was spying on me. It was plain as day that ol' Kyle was doing the cultural dance of the Merrill Lynchkins. For some reason Kyle Rice & Co. was in fear of Hal Blackwell, and he was in rapid motion to protect himself from the perceived threat.

I continued to tell the truth no matter what the question or subject matter, which seemed to just bug the hell out of Kyle Rice.

About two days after this conversation, Bill came up to me as I was standing outside his office waiting on a document from the printer. He put his hand on my back and just smiled at me and said, "Hal, you are an honest man." I took this to mean Kyle Rice and Randy Dennis had been desperately going through my closet in a frantic search for a hidden skeleton, but to no avail.

The following Monday morning, I received a call from Kyle Rice telling me, in his most ominous tone, to clear my calendar on Wednesday because he needed me in Columbia to discuss my practice. It was Kyle's attempt at being intimidating, and he obviously was trying to scare me. Having told the truth and having done nothing wrong, I did not care what he wanted to talk about. He promised to follow up with an e-mail to notify me of exactly what time the inquisition was scheduled to begin. At about three thirty he e-mailed informing me to be there at nine o'clock the next morning.

Intent on being the authoritarian, Kyle had neglected to request a confirm-ing response to his message. Too embarrassed to call or send a follow-up e-mail asking for confirmation, around four o'clock he called the office to ask Lucy if I had received the message. I waited for about thirty minutes before sending him the e-mail he had neglected to ask for. I enjoyed those thirty minutes know-ing Kyle was in Columbia wringing his hands because he had been preparing a barbeque and faced the prospect of having nothing to throw on the grill. It was petty and childish, I know, but the way this whole thing was being handled started to make me feel humiliated and more than just a little defensive.

If Kyle Rice, and by proxy Bill Edmunds, had a problem with me or the way I was doing business, why couldn't they just man up and ask me about it? They were acting like I was some intimidating bully in the schoolyard. The "Golden Rule" course of action, treating someone the way you would want to be treated, would have been to just ask me. They could have just put all the cards on the table and said let's talk about it. In South Carolina an employer can fire an employee for having a bad hair day, so it wasn't about justifying my dismissal.

It all boiled down to the ethos engrained in the culture. Be sneaky, be disingenuous, avoid transparency, always have an excuse, run for cover, don't have any core beliefs worth standing for, never accept responsibility, excel at blame shifting, and be terrified of failing was the code these guys lived by, and I was fast losing respect for every last one of them.

Every compliance officer I have ever met was a wannabe district attorney deep down inside.

When I arrived in Columbia that morning, the office receptionist escorted me to a small conference room located in the management corner. Kyle Rice then introduced me to William E. Goydan, a partner in the law firm of Wolff & Samson, PC, from West Orange, New Jersey. Via speakerphone they introduced me to another attorney who was joining us from his office in New Jersey. Goydan asked me to address him as Bill, and he gestured for me to have a seat in the chair directly across the table from him. He was a handsome, middle-aged guy with blond hair that was cut short, and he looked intelligent. He reminded me a little of the actor Lee Majors except that he wore glasses.

The speakerphone was immediately to my right, and Kyle Rice (who by now was almost in the throes of a mental orgasm), was seated to my left at the end of the table.

Adhering to my philosophy of never, ever let 'em see you sweat, I decided to scoot my chair back from the table a little and lean back in a relaxed position. I was really not anxious because I had not done anything wrong intentionally and positively had not lied about anything.

Having read and studied the silent communications of body language, I adopted a non-confrontational posture with my arms open, intending to relay the message to Bill that my objective was to be as honest and as transparent as possible.

Bill started the conversation by explaining to me that he was not there as my attorney (a fact I had picked up on immediately) and that any information gathered belonged to Merrill Lynch and enjoyed the protection of the attorney/client privilege. He also added that at ten thirty the questioning would be halted so that he could take a scheduled phone call. All of which sounded pretty reasonable to me.

It wasn't long before I discovered that lawyers from New Jersey did not know or care about body language. I could tell by the tone in his voice that Bill was putting no effort in the interpretation of my conciliatory silent messages. I reckoned he was getting paid too much and/or he was smarter than me.

Bill flinched with annoyance when Kyle let it slip that he had been involved with the inspection of my laptop. That prompted Bill to grab the reigns immediately, and with Kyle Rice looking on intently, he started asking the questions exclusively.

The first question out of Bill's mouth was about the desktop computer in my office and how I stored files on it. This caught me off guard, and I tried to answer based on how I perceived the question, but I was not sure I had interpreted the question correctly. I augmented my answer by suggesting that he go look for himself since the firm has unfettered access to every employee's computer. As the words left my lips, I felt foolish because this was certainly not news to Bill Goydan. When it was clear Bill wanted me to answer the question, I knew that Merrill Lynch had sprung for some high-priced legal talent imported from New Jersey to catch me in a lie. He knew damn well how I stored files on my computer. If he was here to catch me in a lie, all I could do was mentally wish him good luck because he was going to need it.

Right away it was clear this was no meeting with the intent of educating anyone about my practice, which in my book made Kyle Rice out to be a coward. Upon reflection, expecting Kyle to send an e-mail on Monday asking me to be in Columbia on Wednesday so that Merrill Lynch could have an attorney from New Jersey endeavor to prove I was a liar would have given me an unfair advantage. Apparently I was so frightening to Kyle Rice and Bill Edmunds they reached into the well and pulled out the venerable legal talents of Wolff & Samson, PC. It's no fun to work for cowards who are ever-vigilant to cover an exposed backside.

After inadvertently letting me know what the game was all about with the technology line of questioning, Bill started to ask questions about ARF and my efforts to provide them access to the Merrill Lynch platform of services. He asked me several open-ended questions that I answered candidly and completely. There was no difference in what was taking place in that conference room and a deposition. This was home turf for Bill, and I knew that at some point along the way he would attempt to make me angry. I reminded myself repeatedly to never let these two see me sweat, always maintaining an even keel, biding my time, consciously waiting on the temperature adjustment that was sure to come.

Promptly at ten thirty, the proceedings ceased so that Bill could take his phone call. Kyle invited me to sit in an office two doors down from the conference room in solitary confinement until court reconvened. My cell had no pictures on the wall, nothing but the starkest furnishing of a desk, the chair I was sitting in, a credenza, two small chairs in front of the desk, and a work station (not online) to keep me company as I waited. I did have my trusty Blackberry though, and as soon as the door closed, I entered Bill Goydan's name in the Google search box. What popped up was impressive: member of the law firm of Wolff & Samson, graduate of University of Richmond (cum laude), Rutgers School of Law (with honors), and on and on. Old Bill was a smart one, all right. I was flattered Merrill Lynch thought so much of me.

Once everyone was back in place, I asked Bill if our conversation was being recorded, and he said that it wasn't. The way he said it made me doubt him.

Bill then did something that disrespected my body language and other conciliatory efforts. He reached behind the conference table and produced three five-inch-thick, three-ring binder notebooks and handed one to me, one to Kyle, and kept one for himself. He was openly going on the attack now.

Before allowing me to open my prize package, he asked me a question that inferred that I had lied to him earlier. At that point my body language did change on purpose, and I pulled my chair up to the table, slowly crossed my arms and rested them on the table in front of me, looked at Bill square in the eye, grill to grill, and said, "That question infers that I have lied to you, and I want you to know that I am offended by that. I am going to answer your question, but for the record, your inference is hogwash."

"But you did lie to us. Why don't you open the notebook to..." and he gave me a number that corresponded to one of the hundred or so tabs sticking out of this vast sea of paper.

We had finally come to the point where Bill was turning up the heat.

When I opened the massive document in front of me, there before my eyes was what looked to be every e-mail I had written in my four years at Merrill Lynch—meticulously organized, labeled, and indexed.

My immediate thought was that Merrill Lynch had paid more for the legal effort to read and categorize my e-mails than they had paid me the previous year.

My next thought was a profound moment of clarity: for the last two weeks I, Hal Blackwell, had been the focal point of this hotshot lawyer's life. I felt like Merrill Lynch had been ripped off by Bill's soap-opera attempt to rile me by calling me a liar followed by the melodrama of springing his surprise on me. I could not wait to see what was in the referenced exhibit.

Out of the corner of my eye I could see Kyle Rice deeply immersed in the scene, and he appeared to be a high-powered Wall Street attorney created in a Walter Mitty episode as he crossed his legs and peered over the top of his book of evidence. I could only see his eyes, his long forehead, and the buzz crew cut on the top of his head. His fascination with the legal gambits and methods he observed was palpable as the vibrations of his biorhythms of love for Bill washed over the table in his direction, inadvertently ricocheting off of me. The exhibit revealed nothing, and the gambit to rile me failed.

These two, and apparently the whole apparatus of the firm, had become convinced that I had accepted payment from ARF outside of Merrill Lynch, encouraged my clients to invest in ARF, and committed various other outrageous transgressions.

At a minimum, they were going to prevent me from leaving Merrill Lynch unscathed. I was at a huge disadvantage playing on this field. They knew it but I also knew it.

Since one of their primary accusations was that I acted as a lobbyist because I accompanied the ARF officials to Washington, I was inclined to believe they wanted to give me a good whuppin' before I hit the road. The fact that I had sent detailed accounts of my activities via e-mail to all levels of management made no difference and was irrelevant to the purposes of this little get-together.

All of their accusations were groundless with the exception of my failure to dot the i's and cross the t's before my trip to Georgia to speak at the biofuels conference. Since I had not solicited any accounts or discussed any Merrill Lynch products on the trip, I didn't bother to get permission from management. My presentation at the conference was on the U.S. Treasury yield curve. Delivered at three thirty after a big lunch, my presentation was a real stem-winder. Of the fifty or so people in the room, the ten who were awake when I started were asleep by the time I finished.

Still, it was a mistake, and I was wrong, so I owned up to it. But that's not what they wanted me to own up to.

About three or four more questions into his progression Bill asked me if I had a copy of the ARF prospectus saved on my desktop computer. This time my answer was steadfastly, "Let's go next door and sign on to the system and see." He repeated his question, and I repeated my answer. He then said to turn to exhibit twenty-five. I did, and lo and behold! There was a copy of the prospectus in question. Again, this was clearly an attempt to make me angry.

They both paused to gauge my reaction. I looked at the both of them and calmly said, "Hey, look guys, it is obvious that you are here to build some kind of case against me, and I am starting to feel trapped."

In negotiating parlance this is the classic response to two guys playing good cop/bad cop on you. While the give-and-take was not classic good cop/bad cop,

Bill's tactics closely resembled that dynamic, and the only way to defuse his game was to call it what it was.

Bill was not deterred. In his continuing effort to trip me up, he pressed on with a few more blatant attempts at "gotcha" by asking questions and then producing exhibits that could be construed differently than their true meaning. At one point he threatened, "We are going to call Ag Renewable Fuels."

When I pulled out my Blackberry to give him the number, his bluff was called and he moved quickly on to his next question. I could tell Bill was a deposition aficionado. This was his home field, and he knew every blade of grass.

After his next "gotcha" question, I stopped him again and said, "Every instance you cite is open to interpretation. The way you characterize the events or circumstances by refusing to give them context makes each one appear as though I am running roughshod over company policy. The way these events and circumstances unfolded in reality, and when considered within a sequence of events, makes evident I was acting to bring the highest level of service to the client with all means at my disposal. If you can't prove that I was being compensated outside of Merrill Lynch, and you can't because I wasn't, then you are out of bounds and I question your integrity. Any reasonable person would accept my version of events because I have not lied to you and absent this compensation would have had absolutely no reason to act contrary to the best interests of the firm. In not one of the instances you cite are you able to produce one iota of evidence, nor will you ever be able to produce any evidence, that I in any way profited myself, other than what Merrill Lynch paid me, on ARF's cash management account. I never had any hope of being compensated outside of Merrill Lynch, nor was I made any promises by anyone. In fact, some of the efforts I made cost money directly out of my own pocket. To insinuate that I have a hidden agenda is offensive to my honor."

I was very measured in my tone so as to not appear agitated or sound defensive. My tone was the same as I would use to tell a ten-year-old how to hold a golf club for the first time. I was explaining something to them.

Based solely on my words I could tell Bill felt like he was making headway in his quest to anger me. Encouraged, he immediately pressed on with another question, and I had to stop him again. Calmly I said, "Look, we both know you are trying to build a case against me, so in an effort to be absolutely sure about my answers, if I don't remember exactly what was said and under what circumstances it was said, I am going to say 'I don't recall.' I am just telling you beforehand because I know it is going to make you angry, but that is where we are."

After I had my say, in the truest lawyer fashion I have ever witnessed, Bill immediately went from looking me in the eye to peering down at his list of questions in search of the next bullet and fired away.

I fired back, "I don't recall." And so it went for about ten minutes.

When Walter Mitty caught on that my answers were going to be uninformative, he mustered up the gumption to ask a couple. Unlike Bill, Kyle seemed to be edified by my "I don't recall" response to his questions as though it was proving his point. He asked me about whom and what time of day I met with folks on my second trip to Washington. When I said, "I don't recall the name of everyone in the room nor the daily agenda." Kyle looked over to Bill hoping for an attaboy and leaned back in his chair, relishing a moment he was sure to relive later that night with some friends over a beer.

I was turning the tables on Bill, and his frustration showed. "Come on, Hal, that was only two weeks ago."

"I am sorry, Bill. I am simply not prepared to answer the question, so to be on the safe side I have to say I don't recall."

Clearly aggravated, he said, "I am going to have to make a recommendation to someone about my assessment of this situation."

At that point I really did not have a decision to make. My die was cast. I had to stand on my actions and my motives and accept my fate. They were falsely accusing me of something I had not done, and only time would reveal what their motive really was. There was nowhere else for me to move except to admit to something I did not do. The chances of that were negative.

Bill quickly caught himself but not before revealing a tidbit of monumental importance. He said, "I just don't want to have to report that in the internal investigation you were uncooperative."

There it was. Even a novice chess player like me could recognize that checkmate. It was damned if I do and damned if I don't. Old Bill Goydan had indeed earned his Merrill Lynch paycheck. For all my commitment to honesty and my bravery under fire, the deck had been stacked against me before I left my house in Blueberg that morning, probably even before Kyle sent that e-mail on Monday. If I tried to defend myself on Bill's home turf, he would twist my words so that it would appear I had lied and thereby produce prima facie evidence of my guilt. My ability to avoid playing into this trap forced Bill to play his trump card, which was to claim I was uncooperative. As all good lawyers do—and make no mistake, Bill is a great lawyer—he was playing both ends against the middle.

In a final bit of irony, it is worthy to note that all situations involving disputes between brokers and member firms (Merrill Lynch is a member firm) go before FINRA for resolution. Bill Goydan is an arbiter at FINRA. I would say ol' Billy has his backside pretty well bundled. If that were not enough, Merrill Lynch has all of my e-mails and I have none, which includes Kyle Rice's note in August thanking me for my cooperation in sending my computer to Billy. What do you think the chances are of that e-mail ever seeing the light of day? Lest you think these hard-ballers forgot anything, the courts have ruled that member firms have no liability for statements made to FINRA. Merrill Lynch could accuse me of being an axe murderer at FINRA and face no consequences. I could see a BOHICA[7] looming in my not-too-distant future.

After Bill had finished his questioning, it was one thirty; we had been at this for four and a half hours. I was again escorted into my holding cell. After twiddling my thumbs for about forty-five minutes I thought about making a break for it, but the Columbia Merrill Lynch office is a maze and I was not sure of the way out.

I really didn't think they would fire me, but the amount of money invested in Bill and the review of my e-mails meant Merrill Lynch was either unsure about something or very sure about everything (from their perspective). Bill's price tag worried me more than just a little. I wanted to stay with Merrill Lynch, but my treatment had been inexcusable, which added to my ambivalence over the prospect of being divorced from the firm.

Bill had to catch a flight out of Pleasantburg, so as he drove to the airport he planned to call Kyle back to discuss the matter. I sat for one hour while the management team decided my future. To this day I am unaware of who was involved in the discussion. I know that Scott Hotham (the complex manager in Charlotte), Bill Edmunds (the area manager in Columbia), Bill Mitchell (my office manager in Blueberg), and Kyle Rice were all talking to Bill Goydan as he drove up I-26. I wonder if Don Plaus was consulted. If I were a betting man, I would wager yes.

At the end of an hour, Kyle Rice and Bill Edmunds walked into my cell and delivered the bad news. In his best mortician's voice Kyle said, "Hal, I'm sorry but we are going to have to let you go. We need your keys to the office. You have violated Federal lobbying laws and other regulations while refusing to cooperate with our internal investigation. Our lawyer did not feel like you were telling him the truth."

---

[7] BOHICA is a medical acronym for Bend Over Here It Comes Again.

Kyle had graduated from lawyer to judge and jury.

Bill Edmunds said, "If there was a discussion we could be having that might change our decision, we would be having it. I know you claim that you were just providing your client with superior service, but we don't agree."

These morons were firing me for doing my job. They were so steeped in a putrid culture they were blind to what they were doing. I had broken no Federal lobbying laws or violated any regulations (a fact later confirmed by my legal team). The allegations, the interrogation, and the subsequent execution were a cover for their attempt to cut me off before I made a move to the competition.

Bill Mitchell knew I wasn't going to the competition because I had told him so. Bill knew me to be a man of my word. If I said I wasn't going, I wasn't going. The only problem was that these buffoons couldn't distinguish between truth and fiction. You can tell a lot about a person or an organization by the motives they ascribe to you. As the old saying goes, it takes one to know one. Well, I was a truth-teller, a hard worker, and an income producer, yet they sure as heck didn't know me from Adam's housecat. They had become convinced in their paranoia that I was on my way out the door. I had just seen in high definition how the financial services industry addresses such a situation.

I made some comment about some of their managerial inconsistencies, but it was just chatter until I could compose myself. The only response was disbelief. I was just stunned.

I think I said that twice.

At that point I did not want to work for Merrill Lynch anymore. The emotions of the moment made the whole façade and the little people who lived behind it turn my stomach. I got up, stepped from behind the desk, looked Bill Edmunds straight in the eye, and said, "You are making a big mistake." I am sure they thought I meant to go to work for a competitor in Blueberg. I am quite sure they weren't thinking I was going to write this book.

Even at that moment I knew my story would have to be told, and I knew it had to include everything. No one was going to be spared, not even myself.

Kyle reminded me that according to my contract no contact with my clients was permitted and if I did so, it would just make the situation worse.

Bill Edmunds opened the door. Without a word, I walked out of the little office, strode down the path between the cubicles, and cool as a cucumber turned right, opened the door, and walked into a bathroom.

My perfect exit spoiled, I turned to Bill and Kyle, who were following me, and said, "I am trying to find my way out. Can you help me?"

They kindly guided me to a door that led out of the building and into the garage. I opened the door, walked out, and never looked back.

As I walked to my car, emotionally I was numb. What was I going to tell my wife? What was I going to tell my two teenage daughters? I felt terribly embarrassed. Before calling my wife to tell her the news, I prayed.

After praying and before calling, I decided to start my own firm (ten minutes of unemployment was enough). My wife Anita is always best when times are worse. She was great in that moment. Anita knew who I really was and what kind of a man I had become. When she promised to stand by me no matter what, everything else became small.

As I started my ride home, I felt as though I was driving into the great unknown. I felt betrayed by an institution I had defended vigorously on many occasions when the going was tough. I realized how naïve my outlook on the industry had been. My position as a financial advisor had afforded me the opportunity to really help people, and I was going to miss that.

As I drove, I was saddened by thoughts of the people who were going to find out I had been fired by Merrill Lynch. All the people I had asked to trust me were now going to wonder if I had been a con artist. With each name a wave of embarrassment and shame washed over me as if I had committed some crime. As I returned home, I could feel the pain of my humiliation in my bones.

After a period of self-pity and mourning, I had to honestly evaluate the situation. What I had been accused of doing was not in the same league as some misdeeds I had witnessed in my four years at Merrill Lynch. I came to the conclusion that the reason they fired me had to do with my aversion to the culture. I was so alienated from the culture that when I refused to be sneaky and dishonest about my discussions with other firms, Merrill Lynch reacted in a manner demanded by their culture. I don't know if they thought I was taking money under the table from ARF or not. They certainly inferred that they believed that.

These supposedly honest men had taken my devotion to my clients and used it to whipsaw my career. I was an honest guy who was caught in a dishonest culture in which service to the client was secondary. Merrill Lynch's willingness to fabricate charges and make scurrilous allegations against me in an attempt to destroy my career is symptomatic of their chronic disease.

These people, this firm, and this industry have lost their moral compass, and I was not too happy to be paying the price. My heart ached as I thought of my many clients who had depended on me. One stood above the rest. The afternoon I was fired, Bill Mitchell called all of the FAs into the conference room, and my clients were picked over by the system. The mental picture of this made me ill. I knew Coach would call me as soon as he heard. Kyle Rice could kiss my rosy red behind if he thought I was not going to tell my clients exactly what had happened should they call me.

Coach Ford called. We had a great conversation, and a huge burden was lifted. When a member firm at FINRA severs a relationship with a broker, they must file a report outlining the cause. The form is called a U5. I took a copy of my U5 to show Coach Ford because I wanted him to know without a doubt I had not been accused of theft or anything related to my clients' accounts.

As I began to map out future plans, the calling to write this book over-shadowed all other options. Once the hurt and anger subsided, a much bigger picture emerged. The U.S. financial crisis has the investment bankers squarely centered in the regulatory spotlight. The wealth management side of the house, although just as flawed, might escape scrutiny. The powers-that-be had drawn a bead on one, so I decided to draw a bead on the other.

My prayer is that after reading this book those who might affect change within the industry will be called to arms. Their constituencies deserve it, and on their behalf, legislators should demand the sunshine of transparency that will bring meaningful change.

Over the last ten years the wealth management segment of the financial services industry has changed radically. When I was indoctrinated into the cul-ture at Merrill Lynch, I was regaled with recollections of brokers running to the window of the office's cage to enter in orders as Black Monday engulfed the market in October of 1987. There were all the stories of the hot tip or hot stock that endeared brokers to their clients forever. In every office there seemed to be a legendary story of a broker landing a multimillion-dollar account with a lucky phone call.

The Internet's $7 stock trade has destroyed the transactional business model the wirehouse firms counted on to generate cash flow from their inception up until the year 2000. The Internet has also robbed brokers of their information exclusivity. The implementation of the do-not-call list has transformed the way brokers grow their businesses organically.

The entire industry has morphed as the sources of income have shifted. Witness the introduction of the financial advisor. Under the old system, brokers earned money in a straightforward fashion (most of the time), but does anyone really know how a financial advisor is paid? Does anyone know how the financial advisor's firm is paid? To survive, the industry had to be quick and creative to cauterize the two wounds hemorrhaging cash.

The perfect answer has been annuitized assets and their foggy fee structure. These firms and advisors have learned to shave a little here and shave a little there. On the spiral downward in the second quarter of 2008, in an effort to impress analysts, Merrill Lynch bragged about $9 billion of new annuitized assets. A firm can generate significant income shaving around $9 billion.

Does anyone doubt that the management and some of the advisors I have described in this book would take whatever steps were necessary to perpetuate their source of income and influence?

The regulation of the industry is obsolete. Regulators fruitlessly apply standards meant to protect the public under the old ways that wealth management firms earned income. It's like a cop in an '85 Chrysler K car chasing Danica Patrick's Indy car down the backstretch at the Indianapolis Motor Speedway.

The wealth management sophisticates play by new rules and evolve ever-more-clever ways to seize an ever-larger percentage of your savings in a never-ending struggle to fill their coffers with your money. Today's savvy investor is not in a feverish search to identify that once-in-a-lifetime insight that will once and for all best the market. The wise investor in today's global marketplace is on a quest to understand and thwart the secrets of the skim.

22. Epilogue

O f all the shocking aspects of the wealth management business I witnessed (and there were many), the lackadaisical attitude of the lambs being led to the slaughter topped the list. Most investors have no idea how expensive their apathy is.

The state of affairs in the financial services industry is the epitome of the fears which prevented other professions, until recently, from advertising their services. There was a fear that having a good personality would become more lucrative than being a good lawyer, or a good doctor, or a good accountant. The investing public perceives investment advice as a commodity. They purchase it with the same care they might use choosing a local grocery store or home improvement warehouse.

This is an expensive misconception.

Since there are no efficient ways to quantify candidates, advisors have come up with a commensurate recipe for success. By taking on a persona I call the "backslapper," today's successful advisor mixes artificial confidence, faked sincerity, and some fancy lingo to become what the shopper (investor) wants them to be.

Advisors desperately need for prospects to like them more than the competition, for that is the criteria used in today's market for selecting one of the most important individuals in a person's life. We all want to do business with someone we like, but allowing this to be the overriding, determining factor when choosing a professional to serve in a fiduciary capacity is a very poor, not to mention expensive, selection criteria.

Understanding some of the basics of the playing field may help to get you started in the right direction. First off, let me assure you that in order to get the best risk-adjusted return on your investment in today's market, you need a financial advisor. There are just too many investment options and too many sophisticated ways to legitimately manage risk to tackle the job on your own. If you want to get one of those $7 per trade accounts with an online broker and spend time playing the market with mad money, have fun. For your core holdings, get professional advice. A good advisor is worth his or her weight in gold (even at today's prices).

In my opinion, the lesson we learned from the ongoing financial crisis is that the missing element in the financial planning process was the development of a sell strategy. When I realized my clients faced a systemic risk in the economy, I had to improvise. Had I predetermined the warning signs in the market that would make it necessary for clients to go to cash, the process would have been much smoother, more profitable, and much less stressful. As I travel the country campaigning to effect change in the industry, I provide my audience with relevant and current "sell strategies."

It is critical that you and your advisor understand how important it is to avoid taking risks that are nebulous and undefined. To illustrate, consider this arithmetic. Let's use $100,000 for the sake of roundness. If you lose 10 percent, only $90,000 remains. To recoup the $10,000 lost, the investment must rebound 11.11 percent. If your $100,000 were to take a 25 percent hit, the dismal result would be $75,000. To recoup this loss, your investment would need a 33.33 percent boost. In the unfortunate case you endured a 50 percent blow to your $100,000, then the $50,000 remainder would have to reap a 100 percent subsequent return on investment to be at the break-even point of $100,000. The lesson is this: don't lose the money! Money is a lot easier to lose than it is to make! This is why you need an advisor manning the bridge every day.

Since I used arithmetic to demonstrate why it is important to have an advisor, I am going use more arithmetic to show you why having the *right* advisor is crucial. Consider a retirement account with a value of $500,000. If the account were to average 8 percent a year for twenty years, the total account value would be $2,463,401. Changing the return averaged per year to 7.5 percent creates a total of $2,230,408. Finding an advisor willing to provide his services for 1.25 percent a year as opposed to 1.75 percent per year is worth a total over twenty years of $232,992. I can assure you the advisor and his or her firm is well aware of this little calculation. An honest advisor looks to reasonably mitigate client fees whenever possible and always discloses all fees.

No matter how you come to engage your advisor, take the time to understand how the advisor is compensated.

Finding a competent advisor who relies on transactional commissions to feed his family is next to impossible, so don't even try. Only use an advisor who is compensated primarily through annuitized assets such as mutual funds. Due to the use of exchange traded funds (ETFs) in balancing a portfolio, having a second account that is charged a discounted commission is becoming more and more necessary. At Merrill Lynch these accounts are referred to as Merrill Lynch Direct accounts, and the commissions are dramatically lower than any other option. Advisors at Merrill Lynch hate Merrill Lynch Direct accounts because they get paid nothing, and from their wealth management workstation they cannot even see the holdings a client has in the account. I am sure the other wirehouses operate this way as well. The client must ask directly for these accounts and be willing to transact all business online. This is a real money-saver.

As I have tried to hammer home in this book, with annuitized assets the conflict of interest between you and your advisor escalates considerably when the economy and market face systemic issues that require a drastic change in your investment strategy. When the market sends signals that a massive sell-off might be in the offing, your financial advisor, no matter how honest, will have a tendency to advise against selling because his income is substantially reduced if you are holding cash. Again, that is why a predetermined sell strategy is so important. The economy is by no means out of the woods, and assuming that another event like the 2008 episode can't happen again soon is a mistake. You are paying fees for a sell strategy. Make sure one is delivered.

Another revelation you may have picked up on in this book is the "too big to fail" means "too big to tell" characteristic of the large wirehouses. Even an ol' boy from Folksy could figure out that if selling was the right thing to do, a firm with over $2 trillion under management could not advise clients to get out of the market. I assume that people would expect an advisor who had a fiduciary responsibility would be compelled to steer the vulnerable clear of tragedy—not so.

All those millions and millions of dollars spent by the large Wall Street firms for research aren't worth jack squat in a liquidity crisis. A sell recommendation on the market as a whole by one of these firms would crash global markets. Don't consider using one of these firms if you expect or think you deserve such a warning. I recommend finding an independent advisor with an adequate platform who can tell you when to get out. The national wirehouses are better left to the institutional investors and hedge funds. Let the wirehouses pick on someone their own size!

Always remember every piece of propaganda the Wall Street firms put out is primarily focused on impressing the financial advisor corps with the money they are spending to promote them to the marketplace of investors. The high earners, and the teams they form, are the primary concern of the firm's management. The firm is organized to keep them happy.

Special closing tidbit:

Call your advisor and ask for consideration on your annual account fee. These fees range from \$65 to \$200 per year. Each advisor is given a certain amount of discretion with these fees each year. Explain that you have been a good client (for ever how long you have been a good client) and you need a little help this year. It is a great way to put the cost of this book on your broker's tab. He probably owes it to you.

About the Author

After earning his Bachelor of Science in Real Estate Finance from the University of South Carolina, Hal Blackwell founded and subsequently sold Cornerstone Insurance Group, an independent commercial insurance agency, before joining Merrill Lynch as an investment advisor in 2005. The ensuing four years saw many high-profile corporate executives and sports figures trust Hal with their personal fortunes.

In August 2008, well before many of his more experienced peers, he foresaw the coming financial crisis.

In September 2008, Hal counseled his clients to move into cash and other more liquid investments. By taking decisive action, he protected his clients from the sudden and drastic devaluing of investments that occurred in October 2008. The decision was made in spite of the loss of income he suffered personally. This courageous move illuminated a conflict of interest that was to spark controversy within Merrill Lynch.

Having lectured at Clemson University's Graduate School of Entrepreneurship, Hal has shared his experience with executives and students through presentations regarding the principles of win-win negotiation and personal ethics. He is consulted by management on the sale of corporations and corporate decision-making processes. The principal of HE Blackwell Advisors, LLC, he consults on subjects including corporate debt structure, acquisition funding, distressed debt valuation, and capital utilization.

Hal is often asked to lend his expertise interpreting events in the context of market and economic fundamentals within the U.S. and global economy. He carries his message to corporate and consumer audiences by offering thought-provoking and motivational presentations throughout the United States. To attend Hal Blackwell's presentation please visit www.halblackwell.com for event schedules and availability.

Registration and Licensing Services

4802 Deer Lake Drive East, 2nd Floor
Jacksonville, Florida 32246

 **Merrill Lynch**

September 28, 2009

Mr. Harold Blackwell
129 Mabry Drive
Spartanburg, SC 29307

Re: Form U5

Dear Mr. Blackwell;

Please find enclosed a copy of your Form U5 which has been submitted to the appropriate regulatory agencies on your behalf. Please retain a copy of this form for your records. Please be informed that if your AG/RA is not registered within one year from the termination date, you may need to retake the exam.

In addition, please be advised that you are required to maintain a current address with FINRA. In the event that a FINRA firm no longer employs you and your residence changes, you will have to send notification of such change to:

FINRA
Attn: Correspondence Department
P.O Box 9495
Gaithersburg, MD 20898-9495

If you have any questions, please contact your previous manager, or call the Registration Department at 1-866-289-5012, Option #5.

Sincerely,
Registration and Licensing Services

enclosure: Form U5

FORM U5
UNIFORM TERMINATION NOTICE FOR SECURITIES INDUSTRY REGISTRATION

Reference #: 3318919169153D87A	Rev. Form U5
	(05/2009)

Individual Name: BLACKWELL, HAROLD E (5014410)

Firm Name: MERRILL LYNCH, PIERCE, FENNER & SMITH INCORPORATED (7691)

NOTICE TO THE INDIVIDUAL WHO IS THE SUBJECT OF THIS FILING

Even if you are no longer registered you continue to be subject to the jurisdiction of regulators for at least two years after your registration is terminated and may have to provide information about your activities while associated with this firm. Therefore, you must forward any residential address changes for two years following your termination date or last Form U5 amendment to: CRD Address Changes, P.O. Box 9495, Gaithersburg, MD 20898-9495.

1. GENERAL INFORMATION

First Name: HAROLD	Middle Name: E		Last Name: BLACKWELL	Suffix:
Firm CRD #: 7691	*Firm Name:* MERRILL LYNCH, PIERCE, FENNER & SMITH INCORPORATED		*Firm* NFA #:	
Individual CRD #: 5014410	*Individual SSN:* 247-25-8126		Individual NFA #:	Firm Billing Code: 050299

Office of Employment Address

CRD Branch #	NYSE Branch Code #	Firm Billing Code	Address	Private Residence	Type of Office	Start Date	End Date
		050299	MERRILL LYNCH BUILDING 390 EAST HENRY HIGHWAY	N	Located At	07/29/2005	01/11/2006
			SPARTANBURG , SC 29304				
92922	050-299	050-299	390 EAST HENRY HIGHWAY SPARTANBURG , SC 29304 UNITED STATES	N	Located At	07/29/2005	09/16/2009

2. CURRENT RESIDENTIAL ADDRESS

NOTICE TO THE FIRM

This is the last reported residential address. If this is not current, please enter the current residential address.

From	To	Street	City	State	Country	Postal Code
12/2007	PRESENT	129 MABRY DRIVE	SPARTANBURG	SC	US	29307

3. FULL TERMINATION

Is this a *FULL TERMINATION*? ⊙ Yes ○ No
Note: A "Yes" response will terminate ALL registrations with all *SROs* and all *jurisdictions*.

Reason for Termination: Discharged

Termination Explanation:
If the Reason for Termination entered above is Permitted to Resign, Discharged or Other, provide an explanation below:

MR. BLACKWELL'S EMPLOYMENT WAS TERMINATED FOR VIOLATION OF FIRM POLICIES RELATING TO CONTACTING GOVERNMENTAL ENTITIES, OUTSIDE BUSINESS ACTIVITIES,CONFLICTS OF INTEREST,OUTSIDE SPEAKING ENGAGEMENTS,AND FOR NOT BEING FORTHCOMING IN THE FIRM'S INVESTIGATION.

4. DATE OF TERMINATION

Date Terminated (MM/DD/YYYY): 09/16/2009
A complete date of termination is required for *full termination*. This date represents the date the *firm* terminated the individual's association with the *firm* in a capacity for which registration is required.

For *partial termination*, the date of termination is only applicable to post-dated termination requests during the renewal period.

Notes: For *full termination*, this date is used by *jurisdictions/SROs* to determine whether an individual is required to requalify by examination or obtain an appropriate waiver upon reassociating with another *firm*.

The *SRO/jurisdiction* determines the effective date of termination of registration.

6. AFFILIATED FIRM TERMINATION

No Information Filed

7. DISCLOSURE QUESTIONS

IF THE ANSWER TO ANY OF THE FOLLOWING QUESTIONS IN SECTION 7 IS 'YES', COMPLETE DETAILS OF ALL EVENTS OR PROCEEDINGS ON APPROPRIATE DRP(S). IF THE INFORMATION IN SECTION 7 HAS ALREADY BEEN REPORTED ON FORM U4 OR FORM U5, DO NOT RESUBMIT DRPs FOR THESE ITEMS. REFER TO THE EXPLANATION OF TERMS SECTION OF FORM U5 INSTRUCTIONS FOR EXPLANATION OF ITALICIZED WORDS.

Disclosure Certification Checkbox (optional): ☐

By selecting the Disclosure Certification Checkbox, the firm certifies that (1) there is no additional information to be reported at this time; (2) details relating to Questions 7A, 7C, 7D and 7E have been previously reported on behalf of the individual via Form U4 and/or amendments to Form U4 (if applicable); and (3) updated information will be provided, if needed, as it becomes available to the firm. Note: Use of "Disclosure Certification Checkbox" is optional.

Investigation Disclosure

Harold E. Blackwell Jr.
129 Mabry Drive
Spartanburg, SC 29307

November 16, 2009

Investigator Kristin Cristaldi
Financial Industry Regulatory Authority
14 Wall Street, 19th Floor
New York, NY 10005-2101

      Re: STAR #20090199024
               Merrill Lynch, Pierce Fenner & Smith, Inc./Harold Blackwell

Dear Ms. Cristaldi:

This is in response to your letter of October 9, 2009, in which you request my response to the allegations, made by my former employer, Merrill Lynch, Peirce, Fenner & Smith, Inc. (Merrill Lynch), that I was terminated for violation of certain firm policies. I will provide the requested information in the same order as presented in your letter, but specificity may be difficult since the allegations are so vague and I no longer have access to the firm policies that were allegedly violated. I will be happy to supplement this response if I have not adequately addressed your concerns.

Initially, in response to the allegation that my employment was terminated for violation of Merrill Lynch policies relating to (a) contacting government entities, (b) outside business activities, (c) conflicts of interest, and (d) outside speaking engagements, I firmly believe that I have never knowingly or intentionally violated any such policies. I will deal with each allegation separately below, but as background, the allegations appear to arise from my efforts to assist a Merrill Lynch client of mine,_____. The business plan for ____ calls for it to construct four 110 million gallon corn-ethanol plants in the southeast and as a result become a major supplier of ethanol to the southeast U.S. market. If you are interested, you can learn more about ECE at www._____.us.

<u>Contacting government entities</u>. ___ first became a client of Merrill Lynch in April 2008, and at that time had $_ million in working capital, which was placed in a Merrill Lynch account for access by ___ as needed. However, ___ was in need of substantial additional financing for its growth, and, with the full knowledge and often the assistance of others at Merrill Lynch, including my supervisors, I endeavored to assist ___ in securing this financing. Many of us at Merrill Lynch expended considerable effort in exploring different avenues to obtain several hundred million dollars in financing for ___ during the spring and summer of 2008, but these efforts failed when the U.S. financial markets collapsed in September, 2008.

Shortly thereafter we learned of plans in Congress for passage of a stimulus bill, and in January, 2009, with the prior knowledge of my then supervisor, Randy _____, I accompanied ___ officials to Washington, D.C., to observe their efforts to have the stimulus bill changed so as to have corn ethanol designated as an advanced renewable fuels technology. Unfortunately, the ___ officials were unable to persuade government officials to make this change to the stimulus bill, but had their efforts been successful then the financing ___ was seeking might have qualified for a government loan guaranty, which obviously would have substantially increased the likelihood of ___ obtaining the loans it needed. I did attend the meetings with ___ and government officials, but I primarily only observed their interactions and did not substantively participate in the conversations. Upon my return, I reported the results of these meetings to Merrill Lynch and provided a complete list of persons with whom I had contact while in Washington.

In February, 2009, I made a second trip to Washington with ___ officials as they sought to get a federal loan guarantee based on a plan to use biomass to fire the boilers ___ would use to make ethanol. These efforts were also unsuccessful, but _____ _____, my Merrill Lynch Office Manager, was fully aware of this second trip before I left, and afterwards I discussed the results of the trip with him, Scott Hotham and Don Plaus on more than one occasion. I also discussed this trip with Bill Edmonds, the complex manager and Kyle Rice, the complex Compliance Officer, on at least two occasions in early spring, 2009.

Based on the above, I do not believe I violated any Merrill Lynch policy. From the time ___ first became a client, all of our efforts were focused on securing financing for our client because had we been successful it would have

resulted in considerable fees for Merrill Lynch. My presence with ___ officials as they sought federal loan guaranties from government officials was fully
consistent with Merrill Lynch's earlier efforts in this regard, and in my opinion
reflected good, attentive client service, something Merrill Lynch stresses and
prides itself on. Merrill Lynch was fully aware of the trips in question and the
purpose of the trips, and at no time before or upon my return did anyone suggest that the trips might be a violation of some firm policy. All of my efforts as
described above were always taken in the best interests of both the client and
Merrill Lynch, and I believe it is unfair and disingenuous for Merrill Lynch to
now claim otherwise.

Outside business activities. After ECE became my client, I began participating in ECE Board meetings via conference call after I had been elected but
before I accepted a position of the ECE board of directors. This participation
was strictly as ECE's Merrill Lynch Financial Advisor and was done with Merrill
Lynch's full knowledge and permission. The first board meeting I listened to
was in late July, 2009 and, knowing that certain Merrill Lynch policies address
such situations, I discussed the matter with the Merrill Lynch complex Compliance Officer, Sean Blevins. We sent a request for permission to accept this position to the Merrill Lynch home office in New York, and Mr. Blevins instructed
me not to accept the position or participate in the affairs of ECE as a board
member until our request was acted upon by the home office. I followed these
directions, but I was permitted by Mr. Blevins to attend Board meetings in my
capacity as ECE's Merrill Lynch Financial Advisor.

The enclosed letter from the Chief Executive Officer of ECE confirms my
limited role with ECE and should answer any questions in this regard.

I have learned, however, that certain documents prepared by ECE (such as
minutes of Board meetings) designate me as member of the Board of Directors.
I was unaware of these documents at the time they were prepared, and I do not
believe I should be held responsible for errors made by others. I was briefly and
incorrectly identified as an ECE Board member on an internet networking business site, but this too was an inadvertent error. For your information, those
mistakes have since been corrected.

While some misimpressions may have occurred, based on the letter from
ECE it is undisputed that I did not in fact participate in any outside business

activities with ECE while I was employed by Merrill Lynch and therefore this allegation is simply factually incorrect.

Conflicts of interest. I am aware of no conflicts of interest I had while employed by Merrill Lynch. As explained above, I served only in an advisory capacity for ECE, and I never concealed my relationship with ECE from Merrill Lynch, I was never compensated by ECE, and I never engaged in any marketing of ECE to anyone. In fact, I would be surprised if any of my other clients even knew ECE was a client of mine.

Outside speaking engagements. The only outside speaking engagement that has recently been brought to my attention as a concern of Merrill Lynch occurred in July, 2009, when I spoke to the Southeastern Renewable Fuels Conference. Robert Mauney, my Merrill Lynch Officer Manager, was aware of my intention to speak prior to the event, and since the invitation to do so involved a Merrill Lynch client (ECE), I again saw this as an opportunity to provide additional good, attentive client service.

The topic of my speech to this group was the Treasury Yield Curve, and in my talk I attempted to explain to the attendees why the credit market was so tight. While it was known that I was a Financial Advisor employed by Merrill Lynch, I never mentioned, much less discussed, any Merrill Lynch programs, policies, offerings or services.

At no time did anyone at Merrill Lynch express any reservations about my speaking to this group, and no one suggested that to do so would be a violation of any firm policy, presumably because the topic had nothing whatsoever to do with my employer. Again, I believe it is unfair and inaccurate for Merrill Lynch to now allege that this incident violated firm policy.

I hope the above adequately provides the information in the first request in your letter. If not I would be happy to address any other questions or issues.

Regarding the other questions raised in your letter, I was never compensated in any way by ECE for any of my activities with it, I never solicited any customers of Merrill Lynch regarding any matter involving ECE, Merrill Lynch was fully aware of and in fact often encouraged my activities with and on behalf of ECE, and to my knowledge there have never been any complaints by anyone regarding any aspect of my employment with Merrill Lynch.v

Lastly, I believe it is important for you to know the full context of my relationship with Merrill Lynch at the time I was terminated. As explained below, I fear that the firm may be seeking retribution against me through FINRA for activities wholly unrelated to the above issues and I believe FINRA should not be misused in this fashion.

For some months prior to being fired I had repeatedly complained to my supervisors at Merrill Lynch about certain firm practices that I believed were detrimental to the best interests of our clients. Contrary to the advice the firm wanted given, as the market tumbled I moved my clients into stronger cash positions and out of equities. While my compensation certainly suffered, so did that of the firm (at least that portion generated by my accounts), and for this I was severely criticized despite my clients happily surviving the 2009 market crash.

In addition, at least in part because of the turmoil caused when Merrill Lynch was purchased by Bank of America, during this time a number of Merrill Lynch Financial Advisors left and became employed by one of the firm's main competitors. It was rare for a week to go by without a competitor attempting to get me to leave Merrill Lynch and come to work with a new employer. Admittedly I seriously considered this at one time, and I believe Merrill Lynch became aware of this. However, I had decided to remain with Merrill Lynch and I never provided any competitor with any information about my Merrill Lynch accounts and clients.

I believe a strong argument can be made that the true basis for the unwarranted and unsubstantiated allegations made against me by Merrill Lynch is either because I was not considered to be a good Merrill Lynch team player, or, as is probably more likely, concern that I would leave Merrill Lynch for a competitor and take my clients with me, including ECE which, if financing was secured, would be a client that would produce substantial revenue. By smearing me (or attempting to do so), Merrill Lynch would succeed in both punishing me personally for my perceived "disloyalty" and make it less likely any client would follow me anywhere. While I have no immediate plans to seek employment as a Financial Advisor or solicit ECE's account for anyone, Merrill Lynch's efforts are simply wrong and I hope FINRA will not be a party to these efforts.

I appreciate the extension of time you gave me to provide this response, and if you have any questions or if you are in need of any additional information, please feel free to contact me.

Sincerely,

Harold E. Blackwell, Jr.

Made in the USA
Lexington, KY
06 March 2011